KEYS *to* PRESERVING YOUR DESTINY

THE DOORWAY TO TRIUMPHANT AND ABUNDANT LIVING

GEORGE MFULA

Keys to Preserving Your Destiny

ISBN: 978-0-6483625-1-7

Published by Faith Digest Media Library

For further information or permission, please contact:

Faith Digest Media Library
Rise and Walk Church Inc.
SYDNEY AUSTRALIA
Phone: +61. 425-338-781
Email: riseandwalk@hotmail.com
Website: www.riseandwalk.org.au

Text design by: Sriraman Ramachandran
Cover design by: George Mfula
Interior design by: Sriraman Ramachandran

National Library of Australia Cataloguing - in - Publication Data:

Author: Mfula George –
Title: Keys to Preserving Your Destiny(pbk)
ISBN: 978-0-6483625-1-7
Subjects: Christian Living / Religious Book

Contents

Mandate

God once said to me, "Go! I'm sending you like I sent Moses, my prophet, to liberate my people from all oppressions of the devil through the preaching and teaching of the word of faith. Raise the foundations of many generations, prophesy over them and school them into supernatural knowledge, wisdom and exploits; impart into them my power and wisdom; release them into their glorious and unparalleled destinities."

Introduction

Keys to Preserving Your Destiny is written to help you locate and secure your destiny in Christ Jesus for unparalleled results. I believe after you finish reading this book, you will be ready to fulfill your destiny in a grand style. God already set your destiny in motion before you were even born. Hence, your destiny and existence here on earth is not strange to God. However, if you don't know your destiny, life becomes very hard.

Apart from that, you may ask a question, "But what is destiny, Pastor George?" Well, destiny is the divine assignment which God has put into your life to serve the purposes of His kingdom. Look, before your life takes off to dimensions of success, you have to know what destiny is all about! Destiny has nothing to do with making money or the more. Instead, it has everything to do with your divine purpose in Christ Jesus.

There cannot be greatness without discovering your destiny first. The Word of God is one tool that could help you discover, preserve, and fulfill your destiny. I believe the number one enemy of your destiny is the devil. Hence, don't be ignorant—he is the enemy of your soul and destiny. We are at war! While you are looking for destiny fulfillment, he is also looking for an opportunity to stop it. God forbid!

Ephesians 6:10-12

Finally, my brethren, be strong in the Lord and in the power of His might. Put on the whole armor of God, that you may be able to stand against the wiles of the devil. For

> we do not wrestle against flesh and blood, but against principalities, against powers, against the rulers of the darkness of this age, against spiritual hosts of wickedness in the heavenly places.

Did you know that each time the devil comes against your marriage, vision, ministry, finances, career, family and health, he is not after anything else, but your destiny? That's why I am convinced today that your destiny is very important to God, more than you may imagine or think. Look, for your life and destiny to be fulfilled will always need a vigilant spirit. Yes, don't watch the devil do whatever he wants in your life. No!

In the year 2006, God spoke to me about the importance of destinies in as far as saving the lost is concerned. God designed your destiny to preserve millions of people around you from going down to Hell. Hence, what you do with your destiny today will eventually affect those millions of people waiting for you to rescue them from destruction. It is time to arise and pursue your destiny with every strength and passion in Christ Jesus. Stay blessed.

CHAPTER 1

Bible-Generated Faith

Faith Versus Destiny

It will always take Bible-generated faith to preserve your destiny in Christ Jesus. Without a doubt, you have a colourful and God-ordained destiny, but you need persistent faith to have it preserved, established, and fulfilled.

Romans 10:17

So then faith *comes* by hearing, and hearing by the word of God.

What is Faith?

(1) Faith is the substance of things hoped for, and the evidence of things not seen (Hebrews 11:1-2). It is also the obedience you show to God's Word or commandments. For example, the account of Noah in the Bible shows us exactly what Bible generated faith is all about. You can't claim to be walking in faith if you can't even obey God's Word. Faith is not just a definition or confession, but obedience to God's Word.

Hebrews 11: 7

By faith Noah, being divinely warned of things not yet seen, moved with godly fear, prepared an ark for the saving of his household, by which he condemned the world and became heir of the righteousness which is according to faith.

Genesis 6:22

Thus Noah did; according to all that God commanded him, so he did.

Without doubt, faith has the power to preserve your destiny from corruption, stagnation, and pollution. Hence, it doesn't matter how big or colorful your destiny is in Christ Jesus. Without Bible generated faith, it won't find fulfilment. Many beautiful people, including Christians, have turned their backs against faith in order to live by the system of this world. It is such a sad development and unpleasing to God our Father in Heaven.

I remember when I got enrolled in a Bible College to study Pastoral Ministry, the entire journey was a journey of faith. Nothing else! I knew studying in Bible College was part of my destiny in God's divine agenda. My destiny was to become a great man of

God—a revivalist across the nations of the earth. However, to have had achieved that, I needed Bible generated faith—a faith that was Word birthed and driven.

I'm glad to say my faith in God and His Word worked for me in amazing ways. Well, was it that easy? Of course not! I had so many challenges because of my prophetic calling into ministry. For this reason, any dream, vision, or destiny that needs to see fulfilment, faith, is non-negotiable. Hence, I gave myself to the Word of God, prayer, and fasting. If you don't take responsibility in your life to grow your faith, no one will do it for you.

Every destiny or vision needs preservation in one way and another in order to march forward. I believe no destiny will ever get fulfilled unless it first gets preserved. There are many people today who are no longer in ministry because of the wickedness of this world. The devil will always fight against your destiny to corrupt it, hence the need for faith. Faith is non-negotiable in preserving and fulfilling your destiny in Christ Jesus.

Mark 9:21-23

So He asked his father, "How long has this been happening to him?" And he said, "From childhood. And often he has thrown him both into the fire and into the water to destroy him. But if You can do anything, have compassion on us and help us." Jesus said to him, "If you can believe, all things *are* possible to him who believes."

If people today can just keep on believing God and His Word, preserving their destinies won't be an issue at all. May you allow the Holy Spirit to grow your faith for preserving your life and destiny in Christ Jesus.

What is Destiny?

Many years ago, God gave me a definition of what destiny is all about. I got excited as I was preaching in our church on a message titled "The Seven Pillars of Destiny." Well, here is the definition of destiny:

"Destiny is a divine assignment God has put into your spirit or life to advance the purposes of His Kingdom."

Every person has a God-ordained destiny in them. Who put it there? Well, God did! The only thing remaining is to discover that destiny in Christ Jesus. Hence, if you are not born again or a child of God, you better first give your life to Jesus. Your relationship with God is the beginning point of destiny discovery, establishment, and pursuit. Meanwhile, let us have a look at the dictionary meaning of the word destiny:

"The events that will necessarily happen to a particular person or thing in the future. It

also means the hidden power believed to control future events; fate."

When you look at the definition of destiny from the dictionary above, it is not incorrect, but incomplete. That is because before you were even born physically, God knew you, chose you, and gave you a destiny. Your destiny is not futuristic or in the future—it is already there waiting for you. Hence, your existence here on earth does not take God by surprise. He knew you before you even existed or stepped into your mother's womb.

Besides, it doesn't matter who you are or where you live as long as you are in Christ Jesus; you have a destiny to discover, preserve and fulfill. The destiny potential within you is strong enough to move the mountains and shake the kingdom of darkness. However, in order for you to preserve and fulfill your destiny in Christ Jesus, you need faith. Bible generated or driven faith cannot get overemphasised in preserving and fulfilling your destiny.

I have seen many people who have had dreams of becoming great people, but nothing happened. Well, what happened? I believe most of the times the problem is lack of faith to preserve their destinies in Christ Jesus. When you have faith, your destiny gets activated and enhanced for unparalleled results. It is one thing to have a destiny and another to have it fulfilled—hence the need for Bible generated faith.

Mark 11:23-24

For assuredly, I say to you, whoever says to this mountain, 'Be removed and be cast into the sea,' and does not doubt in his heart, but believes that those things he says will be done, he will have whatever he says. Therefore I say to you, whatever things you ask when you pray, believe that you receive *them,* and you will have *them.*

3 Reasons Faith is Vital in Preserving Your Destiny

Hebrews 11:30-34

By faith the walls of Jericho fell down after they were encircled for seven days. By faith the harlot Rahab did not perish with those who did not believe, when she had received the spies with peace. And what more shall I say? For the time would fail me to tell of Gideon and Barak and Samson and Jephthah, also *of* David and Samuel and the prophets: who through faith subdued kingdoms, worked righteousness, obtained promises, stopped the mouths of lions, quenched the violence of fire, escaped the edge of the sword, out of weakness were made strong, became valiant in battle, turned to flight the armies of the aliens.

(1). Faith Supplies the Power

2 Peter 1:3

As His divine power has given to us all things that *pertain* to life and godliness, through the knowledge of Him who called us by glory and virtue.

In order to preserve and fulfill your destiny in a grand style, you need the power of God. I believe without God's power in your life, you can't become anything in this world. Besides, it is Bible generated faith that supplies the power to preserve your destiny. Friends, you need power to humiliate all devils fighting against your destiny today. Hence, don't get casual about your destiny — instead, engage yourself in a fight of faith.

Ephesians 6:12 (AMP)

For our struggle is not against flesh and blood [contending only with physical op-

> ponents], but against the rulers, against the powers, against the world forces of this [present] darkness, against the spiritual *forces* of wickedness in the heavenly (supernatural) *places*.

In life, it is okay to have an opinion—you may have an opinion about anything in this world. You may even say, "Jesus is there for me and the grace of God is sufficient for me." Of course, that is indisputable — we can't argue or do anything about it. However, it takes a resilient spirit of faith in order for you to fulfill your destiny. We live in a wicked world—thus you cannot neglect God's power at anytime in your life.

The amount of evil fighting your destiny today is rampart and diabolic. It is for this reason you and I need the power of God to establish our dominion walk. What you don't confront, you can't conquer, no matter your opinion. Look, there were 12 tribes in Israel, but only 5 received their inheritance. What went wrong? That was because what you don't pursue, you can't possess, and what you don't confront, you can't conquer.

Joshua 18:1-4

Now the whole congregation of the children of Israel assembled together at Shiloh, and set up the tabernacle of meeting there. And the land was subdued before them. But there remained among the children of Israel seven tribes which had not yet received their inheritance. Then Joshua said to the children of Israel: "How long will you neglect to go and possess the land which the Lord God of your fathers has given you? Pick out from among you three men for *each* tribe, and I will send them; they shall rise and go through the land, survey it according to their inheritance, and come *back* to me.

Our destinies from God cannot fulfil themselves at all. No! Hence the need for destiny preservation, establishment, and pursuit. Of course, you need to put up a fight of faith in order to fulfil your destiny in Christ Jesus.

2 Timothy 4:6-8

For I am already being poured out as a drink offering, and the time of my departure is at hand. I have fought the good fight, I have finished the race, I have kept the faith. Finally, there is laid up for me the crown of righteousness, which the Lord, the righteous Judge, will give to me on that Day, and not to me only but also to all who have loved His appearing.

(2). Faith Supplies the Grace

Look, the reason we need faith to preserve our destinies is because faith supplies the grace. Some people are so smart that they even ignore God's grace in pursuing their destiny. Each time God's grace gets ignored in fulfilling destiny, disgrace comes in. Life without God's grace becomes miserable and a burden to bear. How far you go or excel in life will always be a function of God's grace at work in your life — nothing else!

It doesn't matter your title, race, or how big your destiny is, without God's grace, you are nothing. I have met proud people who never mention God's grace in their lives at all—that is the human nature. God forbid! Without doubt, we all need God's grace to locate, enhance, pursue, and fulfill our destinies. I believe the day I will remove or ignore God's grace in my life that is the day my life will sink and become dung.

1 Corinthians 15:9-11

For I am the least of the apostles, who am not worthy to be called an apostle, because

> I persecuted the church of God. But by the grace of God I am what I am, and His grace toward me was not in vain; but I labored more abundantly than they all, yet not I, but the grace of God *which was* with me. Therefore, whether *it was* I or they, so we preach and so you believed.

I urge you to forget about how creative, intelligent, or famous you are today. It takes God's grace to run your race here on earth. In fact, grace is divine favour or help from God. You and I need the help of God to live our dreams here on earth or in the land of the living. Do not remove God from your daily schedule in order to pursue your goals or destiny. It is a risk! It is something you have to take seriously in your life as a child of God.

Many people have become disoriented in life because God's grace is no longer their language or vocabulary. The grace of God is non-negotiable in pursuing your destiny in Christ Jesus. I believe there is no devil or demon that can stand the grace of God at work in your life. Now, for you to have access to that grace or help of God, you need faith—faith is the access point or key to the grace of God in your life.

> **Romans 5:1-2**
>
> Therefore, having been justified by faith, we have peace with God through our Lord Jesus Christ, through whom also we have access by faith into this grace in which we stand, and rejoice in hope of the glory of God.

Today, if you see the lame walk, the sick healed, the blind eyes open, just know that the grace of God is at work. God's grace is crucial to fulfilling your destiny in Christ Jesus. Never rely on your human strength or intelligibility. No! You must always reach out to God by faith to access

His grace. Faith is the only way or channel available to access God's grace in our lives. Hence, each time you despise God's grace, that is the end of your life.

(3). Faith Activates Your Destiny

I have been in meetings where the atmosphere was so dead, like a rock. No one had faith even to receive anything from God. No presence of God at all! Then, suddenly, after preaching the Word of God, the atmosphere got charged with faith. Without doubt, the activation of faith and God's presence comes from God's Word. It doesn't matter how dead your destiny is today, just grow your faith and your destiny will get activated for fulfilment.

Acts 14:8-10

And in Lystra a certain man without strength in his feet was sitting, a cripple from his mother's womb, who had never walked. *This* man heard Paul speaking. Paul, observing him intently and seeing that he had faith to be healed, said with a loud voice, "Stand up straight on your feet!" And he leaped and walked.

In the above Scripture, when Paul preached God's Word, faith got activated in the crippled man's life. Hence, Paul did not waste time—Instead, he asked the crippled man to rise and walk right there and then. The man's condition was severe, because He was born crippled from his mother's womb. Now, could you imagine some things this man endured in his life being a crippled man? However, God turned his entire life into joy unspeakable by His glorious power.

In the same way, your destiny may look weak and nothing today, but please don't give up! Not only that, you may even no longer believe in yourself or destiny. Well, I pray you won't walk by sight, but by faith in Christ Jesus. You have to come to a place in your life where nothing moves you, except God's Word. I believe faith will always activate your destiny in Christ Jesus for fulfilment. Lack of faith in your life leads to destiny frustration.

Sad to say, some Christians, even pastors who used to be ministry are no longer in ministry today. What happened? Well, when things got tough, they gave up on following God's plan for their lives. Listen, faith will always correct anything that has gone wrong in your life. It has the power to give you a new beginning in Christ Jesus. My prayer is that each time life becomes tough, you won't give up at all. Sorry, giving up is not in God's divine system at all.

Proverbs 24:16 (AMP)

For a righteous man falls seven times, and rises again, But the wicked stumble in *time of* disaster *and* collapse.

You don't give up just because things did not work out for you. No! It is time for you to get up and activate your faith for destiny fulfilment. There is nothing powerful in the journey of life, like being persistent in your faith and walk with God. Hence, each time you fall, don't listen to the devil's suggestions of any kind. The devil's major mission today on earth is to steal, kill and destroy, so don't allow him.

Ephesians 4:26-27

"Be angry, and do not sin": do not let the sun go down on your wrath, nor give place to the devil.

Revelations 12:7-9

And war broke out in heaven: Michael and his angels fought with the dragon; and the dragon and his angels fought, but they did not prevail, nor was a place found for them in heaven any longer. So the great dragon was cast out, that serpent of old, called the Devil and Satan, who deceives the whole world; he was cast to the earth, and his angels were cast out with him.

There was no place found for the devil in Heaven, so don't give the devil a place in your life or destiny. I pray God will rekindle your life, destiny and aspirations once again in Christ Jesus. No devil will stop it!! Jesus once said in the following Scripture:

John 14:30

I will not speak with you much longer, for the ruler of the world (Satan) is coming. And he has no claim on Me [no power over Me nor anything that he can use against Me].

God bless you as you locate and fulfill your destiny in Christ Jesus.

Destiny Prayer 1

"Lord, help me release my destiny, gift and talent in Christ Jesus for destiny preservation and fulfillment."

(James 1:17 NKJV)

CHAPTER 2

The Name of Jesus

Matchless Power

Philippians 2:9-11

Therefore God also has highly exalted Him and given Him the name which is above every name, that at the name of Jesus every knee should bow, of those in heaven, and of those on earth, and of those under the earth, and *that* every tongue should confess

> that Jesus Christ *is* Lord, to the glory of God the Father.

How can the name of Jesus preserve your destiny? Well, in this case, preserving your destiny may imply protecting, safeguarding, nourishing and conserving. There was a time in the Bible when Jesus prayed for His disciples that His name would protect them. In the same way, today, the name of Jesus can preserve your life, destiny, ministry, business, and family. Besides, you don't need to add anything to the name of Jesus. It is powerful by itself!

John 17:11-12

> I will remain in the world no longer, but they are still in the world and I am coming to you. Holy Father, protect them by the power of your name, the name you gave me, so that they may be one as we are one. While I was with them, I protected them and

kept them safe by that name you gave me. None has been lost except the one doomed to destruction so that Scripture would be fulfilled.

With the name of Jesus in your life, just know that your destiny is safe. The name of Jesus is not for show or a ritual practice that gets used to end lunch or dinner prayers. No! The name has matchless power and grace to preserve your destiny from corruption of any kind in this world. However, using the name of Jesus without the revelation of God's Word will not produce any results in your life. Please, don't make that mistake at all!

Mark 16:16-18

He who believes and is baptized will be saved; but he who does not believe will be condemned. And these signs will follow those who believe: In My name they will cast out demons; they will speak with new

> tongues; they will take up serpents; and if they drink anything deadly, it will by no means hurt them; they will lay hands on the sick, and they will recover.

The name of Jesus is an all-around winning ticket for unstoppable progress for every child of God.

Joel 2:32

> And it shall come to pass *That* whoever calls on the name of the Lord Shall be saved. For in Mount Zion and in Jerusalem there shall be deliverance, As the Lord has said, Among the remnant whom the Lord calls.

One of my mentors, Bishop David Oyedepo, shared a testimony of how God preserved him and his wife from a fatal accident. There was going to be a head-on collision with an oncoming vehicle as they drove along a narrow bridge. Now, as the accident was about to take place, his wife called upon the name of Jesus twice. Then, the Bishop responded and said, "mentioning that name *once* is enough." Yes, there is power in the name of Jesus.

I pray that your destiny will not suffer stagnation or destruction anymore. You need nothing more than the name of Jesus — that name is enough! Never give room in your life to wizards, witches, powers of darkness, or cosmic powers through fear. You have the name above all names at your disposal—get up use that name in faith. I bet you the name of Jesus has supernatural power to stop all demonic activities in your life.

However, the extent to which the name of Jesus works for you is determined by your faith and spiritual understanding. This is because, without faith and understanding, nothing will happen in your life. With understanding and faith comes boldness, that the devil can't stand. The entire demonic world today can't stand the name of Jesus. The name of Jesus is our covenant security against all devils, demons, evil spirits, and powers of darkness.

> **Philippians 2:9-11**
>
> Therefore God also has highly exalted Him and given Him the name which is above every name, that at the name of Jesus every knee should bow, of those in heaven, and of those on earth, and of those under the earth, and that every tongue should confess that Jesus Christ is Lord, to the glory of God the Father.

Confidence is Non-Negotiable

Confidence in the name of Jesus is faith at another level of existence. That is why having faith without confidence is not enough—you must make sure your faith graduates to supernatural confidence. Demons won't bow down to you just because you are a Christian. No! You need the confidence of faith in the name of Jesus to preserve your destiny. For example, the three Hebrews boys in Babylon had unusual confidence in God.

Daniel 3:16-18

Shadrach, Meshach, and Abed-Nego answered and said to the king, "O Nebuchadnezzar, we do not need to answer you in this matter. If that *is the case,* our God whom we serve is able to deliver us from the burning fiery furnace, and He will deliver *us* from your hand, O king. But if not, let it be known to you, O king, that we do not serve your gods, nor will we worship the gold image which you have set up."

What you hear in the Scripture above from the Hebrew boys is the spirit of confidence in God and His name. That is why faith is having absolute confidence in God, His

Word, and name. You can't preserve your destiny without supernatural confidence at work in your life. One man of God shared a testimony where a robber pointed a gun at him and said, "I will shoot you," but the man of God replied and said "No, you can't." That was it!

Eventually, the robber dropped his gun and ran away in terror. Without doubt, no demon, devil, witch, wizard, or even a robber can stand the name of Jesus. When the man of God stood in faith in the name of Jesus, the thief ran away in confusion and terror. Look, each time confidence is at work in your life, angels get released to protect you. Hence, don't treat the name of Jesus with levity, otherwise it won't work for you.

Acts 3:1-10

Now Peter and John went up together to the temple at the hour of prayer, the ninth *hour.* And a certain man lame from his mother's

> womb was carried, whom they laid daily at the gate of the temple which is called Beautiful, to ask alms from those who entered the temple; who, seeing Peter and John about to go into the temple, asked for alms. And fixing his eyes on him, with John, Peter said, "Look at us." So he gave them his attention, expecting to receive something from them. Then Peter said, "Silver and gold I do not have, but what I do have I give you: In the name of Jesus Christ of Nazareth, rise up and walk." And he took him by the right hand and lifted *him* up, and immediately his feet and ankle bones received strength.
> 8 So he, leaping up, stood and walked and entered the temple with them–walking, leaping, and praising God.

In the above Scripture, it was faith in the name of Jesus that made the man walk. I have seen many people use the name of Jesus with doubt, and nothing happens. I would rather you took some time to study God's Word, and understand the power behind the name of Jesus. Then, when you use it in faith, that power will get released to set the captives free. The power in the name of Jesus is eminent to your faith.

Apart from that, the name of Jesus is the badge of authority that Jesus left for us here on earth—the Church. If you want to produce results in your life of another order, then add faith to the name of Jesus. Without Bible generated faith, your confessions of the name of Jesus won't work for you. However, there is unmatched power in the name of Jesus we are yet to see. All we need is solid faith in that glorious and powerful name.

Acts 19:13-16

Then some of the itinerant Jewish exorcists took it upon themselves to call the name of the Lord Jesus over those who had evil spirits,

> saying, "We exorcise you by the Jesus whom Paul preaches." Also, there were seven sons of Sceva, a Jewish chief priest, who did so. And the evil spirit answered and said, "Jesus I know, and Paul I know; but who are you?" Then the man in whom the evil spirit was leaped on them, overpowered them, and prevailed against them, so that they fled out of that house naked and wounded.

I believe in the above account, the seven sons of Sceva did not have the revelation of the name of Jesus. Look, you can not walk in higher realms of faith without the revelations of God's Word. Not only that, but you cannot walk in supernatural confidence without faith. It is a chain of spiritual elements — one element leads to another. Hence, when they used the name of Jesus, things did not go well for them. It was horrible!

Besides, I don't even know if they were believers in God's Word or the name of Jesus. Of course, there is a lot to question about them! Maybe you have tried to use the name of Jesus, but there is no power to match your command or results. Well, one thing I know is that the name of Jesus still works today as it did 2000 years ago! Just build up your spiritual muscles or authority by growing your faith in the Word of God.

Many years ago, they brought to me a young boy who needed urgent prayer. He was going through a serious and terrible satanic oppression. According to him, a person would come with a big stick to whip him at anytime. Unfortunately, that person whipping him was invisible to the public—it was such a spiritual attack and operation. Sad to say, the boy quit school and was just at home with his family in agony.

Now, the very day they brought him to me, I stood in the name of Jesus and commanded with confidence and authority for that demonic oppression to stop. Then I sent him away with a blessing in the name of Jesus. Two weeks later, they came back with a testimony about the deliverance of the young boy. God delivered him from that satanic oppression. There is power in the name of Jesus to restore and rewrite your destiny.

Supernatural Revelation

Proverbs 29:18 AMP

Where there is no vision [no revelation of God and His word], the people are unrestrained, but happy and blessed is he who keeps the law [of God].

What is revelation? It is the things you see when God opens up your spiritual eyes. When God opens up people's spiritual eyes, some will see God's purpose for their lives while others will see the exact plan God has for them. Without doubt, God's revelations will always preserve and establish your destiny in Christ Jesus. The revelations of the Holy Spirit are a must if you want to benefit from the power that is in the name of Jesus.

Look, it is one thing to preach about faith and another for you to see the results of your preaching. It is not the preached Word that preserves your destiny in Christ Jesus, but the one you see and act upon in faith. The revelation of the Word of God flowing in your life will always bring a revolution in your own life. Friends, when you see it, we call that revelation because the Spirit of God has revealed it to your human spirit.

Apart from that, we all know that when the Holy Spirit reveals something to you, it stays in your life. Why? That is because whatever the Holy Spirit does is perfect and permanent in Christ Jesus. The same thing happened to Apostle Peter, when the Holy Spirit gave him a revelation concerning Jesus. Just that one revelation of who Jesus was preserved Peter's destiny and gave him a place in the school of power and success.

Matthew 16: 13-15

When Jesus came into the region of Caesarea Philippi, He asked His disciples, saying, "Who do men say that I, the Son of Man, am?" So they said, "Some *say* John the Baptist, some Elijah, and others Jeremiah or one of the prophets." He said to them, "But who do you say that I am?"

Everyone knew Jesus as the son of David, according to the flesh. However, it took the revelation of the Holy Spirit for Peter to have known that Jesus was the Christ, the Son of the living God. Of course, Jesus was more than just the son of David in the flesh—He is God! In fact, His name is called Wonderful, Counsellor and The mighty God. It will always take the revelation of the Holy Spirit for us to know who Jesus is.

Matthew 16:16-18

And Simon Peter answered and said, 'Thou art the Christ, the son of the living God.' And Jesus answered and said unto him, 'Blessed art thou, Simon Barjona, for flesh and blood hath not revealed it unto thee but my Father which is in heaven. And I say also unto thee that thou art Peter, and upon this rock I will build my church and the gates of hell shall not prevail against it.

With no shadow of doubt, what the church or believers need today is revelation knowledge. There are two types of knowledge. There is what we call *head knowledge,* the knowledge that you learn from school or just anywhere in life. Then, there is also what we call *revelation knowledge,* or the Holy Spirit's knowledge. You can't learn this one from school, but gets revealed to you by the Holy Spirit as a child of God.

For example, I can teach you about faith and how it comes. However, you won't have it just because I taught it. Instead, the Holy Spirit has to reveal it to you personally in your own spirit. When that happens, we call it *revelation knowledge.* It is not coming from your head or from what you know, but from the Holy Spirit. Hence, when revelation hits your life, there will always be a revolution, no matter the case.

Ephesians 1:16-18

Do not cease to give thanks for you, making mention of you in my prayers: that the God of our Lord Jesus Christ, the Father of glory, may give to you the spirit of wisdom and revelation in the knowledge of Him,

> 18 the eyes of your understanding being enlightened; that you may know what is the hope of His calling, what are the riches of the glory of His inheritance in the saints.

The Spirit of revelation is all about destiny preservation and empowerment. I remember in 2007, at about 2 o'clock in the morning, God led me into a deep realm of prayer and worship. Suddenly, I felt power building up in my hands, legs and then a great shaking came upon me. Eventually, I was down on the floor, slain in the Spirit by the power of God. That experience was remarkable and indelible up till now in my own life.

Well, the only thing I was doing was hallowing the name of Jesus with faith, conviction and excitement in my spirit. I believe it is the same power delivering people today in our ministry from satanic oppression. Any spiritual revelation from

God about the name Jesus will always bring change to your life. Things will start working for you in the most perfect way in Christ Jesus. Just remember! The name of Jesus is above every other name!

I pray you will not take the name of Jesus for granted. This name has undeniable and matchless power to rescue your destiny from stagnation, spiritual attacks, reproach, and many more. God bless you as you build your life on God's Word.

Destiny Prayer 2

"Lord Jesus, I surrender my all life, destiny, family, business, marriage, plans, ministry into your Hands because you care for me."

(Psalm 27:1; 1Peter 5:7)

CHAPTER 3

Divine Direction

Discerning God's Voice

The voice of God is not a common thing that you just talk about and never honour. It has majestic power for your restoration, preservation, deliverance, healing and empowerment. Besides, you can't treat it with levity and expect things to change in your own life. No! The majestic voice of God has the power to preserve your life and destiny, no matter what is working against you. I pray you pay attention to God's voice henceforth.

Psalm 81:10-14

I *am* the Lord your God, Who brought you out of the land of Egypt; Open your mouth wide, and I will fill it. "But My people would not heed My voice, And Israel would *have* none of Me. So I gave them over to their own stubborn heart, To walk in their own counsels. "Oh, that My people would listen to Me, That Israel would walk in My ways! I would soon subdue their enemies, And turn My hand against their adversaries.

It is hard to have your destiny preserved if you are disobedient to God's voice. As long as God's voice does not matter to you anymore, then you are not safe at all. Christianity is boring and non-effective if God's voice is not something you treasure. Many Christians are trying to become modernized, even with God's voice. They think God's voice is outdated. Well, if that is your behavior, then you are heading for destruction.

What makes Christianity today alive is the voice of God. We are alive because God speaks to us by His voice. This generation is trying to do away with all the fundamental principles of Christianity, such as baptism, holiness, divine guidance, forgiveness, repentance, faith, resurrection and holy communion. Look, as children of God, we are not called to live by our opinions, but by what pleases God in Heaven!

Many years ago, during my days of prayer and fasting, I attended a church conference. Then, after the meeting was over, I met a young girl who was also at the same conference. Now, after talking to her about the Holy Communion we just had, she then said to me, "Holy Communion, man of God, is not my thing." The response got me astounded and confused. She left me wondering about the destiny and direction of this generation.

I believe Holy Communion, just like divine direction, is crucial to the life of a believer. They are both irreplaceable in the Kingdom of God, no matter your opinion or theology. Of course, you can't modernise the Word of God to suit your lifestyle. This can be the greatest error of the church and Christians today. God's Word is perfect, and it doesn't need any adjustments at all. All it needs is for you and me to obey it. Nothing else!

John 6:53-57

Then Jesus said to them, "Most assuredly, I say to you, unless you eat the flesh of the Son of Man and drink His blood, you have no life in you. Whoever eats My flesh and drinks My blood has eternal life, and I will raise him up at the last day. For My flesh is food indeed, and My blood is drink indeed. He who eats

> My flesh and drinks My blood abides in Me, and I in him. As the living Father sent Me, and I live because of the Father, so he who feeds on Me will live because of Me.

Believe me, you can't do away with Holy Communion, just like you can't do away with the need for divine guidance in fulfilling your destiny. In the above Scripture, Jesus mentioned something powerful saying, ***"Unless you eat the flesh of the Son of Man and drink His blood, you have no life in you."*** Yes, you can't put away the fundamental beliefs of the gospel and expect your life to shine tomorrow. Sorry it doesn't work that way!

Of course, Holy Communion is just as important as divine direction in preserving your destiny in Christ Jesus. What is divine direction? Divine direction is the leading or guidance of God in your life. In fact, divine guidance does not benefit God, but it benefits you. Having direction in life is one step toward destiny fulfilment. There are people today, including Christians, who don't care about the voice of God or His divine leading.

Isaiah 48:17

Thus says the Lord, your Redeemer, The Holy One of Israel: "I *am* the Lord your God, Who teaches you to profit, Who leads you by the way you should go.

If God has promised to lead you into realms of honour, safety, blessings, and abundance, then what are you worried about? God's promises are reliable, perfect and never failing. Take God and His Word as the last entity for your life and destiny. When your life is not changing for any reason, just know the problem is not with God or His Word, but with you. If you obey

God's Word or voice today, there is no way God will leave you stranded.

Deuteronomy 28:1- 6

"Now it shall come to pass, if you diligently obey the voice of the Lord your God, to observe carefully all His commandments which I command you today, that the Lord your God will set you high above all nations of the earth. And all these blessings shall come upon you and overtake you, because you obey the voice of the Lord your God: "Blessed *shall* you *be* in the city, and blessed *shall* you *be* in the country. "Blessed *shall be* the fruit of your body, the produce of your ground and the increase of your herds, the increase of your cattle and the offspring of your flocks. "Blessed *shall be* your basket and your kneading bowl. "Blessed *shall* you *be* when you come in, and blessed *shall* you *be* when you go out.

Genesis 6:22

Thus Noah did; according to all that God commanded him, so he did.

Noah obeyed with delight all that God commanded him to do. Then, he and his entire family got preserved from the flood that wiped out everyone from the face of the earth.

The Power of Divine Direction

Success in life is not to the strong or wise, but to God who shows mercy and grace. If God does not show you the way to go, then you are in trouble. All the ways and directions of God are ways of greatness and success. Wherever God leads you to, just know your destiny will get preserved and flourish. We live in a generation where divine direction is of no use. However, you can choose to be different in life as a child of God.

For example, somebody will just wake up in the morning, and decide to buy a ticket and fly off to the USA. Well, did they hear from God, or did God direct them? Sad to say, with many people today there is no sense of divine guidance at all, hence many destinies are stagnant. Every child of God must always seek God's guidance before doing anything. Otherwise, your life and destiny will amount to zero or nothing.

Isaiah 48:17-18

Thus says the Lord, your Redeemer, The Holy One of Israel: "I *am* the Lord your God, Who teaches you to profit, Who leads you by the way you should go. Oh, that you had heeded My commandments! Then your peace would have been like a river, And your righteousness like the waves of the sea.

Psalm 23:1- 6

The Lord *is* my shepherd; I shall not want. He makes me to lie down in green pastures; He leads me beside the still waters. He restores my soul; He leads me in the paths of righteousness For His name's sake. Yea, though I walk through the valley of the shadow of death, I will fear no evil; For You *are* with me; Your rod and Your staff, they comfort me. You prepare a table before me in the presence of my enemies; You anoint my head with oil; My cup runs over. Surely goodness and mercy shall follow me All the days of my life; And I will dwell in the house of the Lord Forever.

God's leading or direction brings you into the realm of abundance, safety and empowerment. There is no way you can reach your destination if you ignore directions. No matter how educated or popular you are, divine direction is vital to your life and destiny. Each time the devil wants to hijack your destiny, all he will do is to confuse you by giving you his own direction. He will try to obstruct you from God's divine direction in total.

Then, after a few months or even years, you discover you have deviated from God's direction. Hence, no matter how hard life becomes, make you sure you keep your eyes on God's divine leading or guidance. Those who take away their eyes from God's guidance don't go very far in life. I have seen many pastors who began well in ministry but ended up taking a different direction. Some are no longer in ministry. God forbid!

Psalm 32:8-10

I will instruct you and teach you in the way you should go; I will guide you with My eye. Do not be like the horse *or* like the mule, *Which* have no understanding, Which must be harnessed with bit and bridle, Else they

> will not come near you. Many sorrows *shall be* to the wicked; But he who trusts in the Lord, mercy shall surround him.

When you spend exclusive time in God's Word, divine direction will be at your disposal. However, it will take your willingness to follow His supernatural guidance or direction. God will not lead you into destruction or darkness because in Him there is no darkness, but only light. He will not also lead you into lack because in Him there is no poverty. Above all, God does not lead anyone by super-imposition or force—it is all about your choice!

Divine direction is a major requirement for destiny preservation and fulfilment. I believe there is no one nation, kingdom or person here on earth greater than God's guidance. Besides, there is no Bible College or Theological Seminary that will ever teach you divine direction.

Divine direction is something that can't get taught anywhere in this world, but can only get caught in the spirit. This may happen during your prayer and fasting.

Divine direction or guidance will always enable you to know God's plan for your life. Besides, it is possible to be anointed by God, but remain stagnant and frustrated in life. The anointing on your life must not be mistaken for divine direction or guidance. In addition, it is possible to be anointed by God, yet you don't have any direction for your life. King David, despite being anointed by God, was a great seeker of God's direction or guidance.

1 Samuel 30:7-9

Then David said to Abiathar the priest, Ahimelech's son, "Please bring the ephod here to me." And Abiathar brought the ephod to David. So David inquired of the Lord, saying, "Shall I pursue this troop? Shall I over-

> take them?" And He answered him, "Pursue, for you shall surely overtake them and without fail recover all." So David went, he and the six hundred men who were with him, and came to the Brook Besor, where those stayed who were left behind.

Now, one reason Israel took unnecessary years long to reach the Promised Land was because of disobedience. The people were very hard to lead—stiff-necked people per se. They spent unnecessary years wandering about in the wilderness, contrary to God's divine design or guidance. They neglected God's leading, so they ended up stranded in the desert for no reason—the devil is a liar!

There are several instances in the Bible where Israel got stagnant because of disobedience. The same thing is true today: disobedience to God's divine guidance leads to stagnation in life. Look, stagnation is not

God's perfect will for you and me. However, if disobedience stands in your way, there is nothing God can do about it. Besides, God can't lead people who don't trust Him and are not ready to submit to Him.

Jeremiah 17:5-6

Cursed *is* the man who trusts in man And makes flesh his strength, Whose heart departs from the Lord. For he shall be like a shrub in the desert, And shall not see when good comes, But shall inhabit the parched places in the wilderness, *In* a salt land *which is* not inhabited.

Putting confidence in man or anything else other than God brings your life down. It affects your destiny, direction and your entire well-being. You become like a parched shrub in the desert that lacks growth and fruit. However, that will not be your portion in the name of Jesus. God wants the best for your life and destiny at all times. He wants to honour your life by His guidance. I believe all the plans of God are for our good.

Jeremiah 29:11-12 AMP

> For I know the plans and thoughts that I have for you,' says the Lord, 'plans for peace and well-being and not for disaster, to give you a future and a hope. Then you will call on Me and you will come and pray to Me, and I will hear [your voice] and I will listen to you.

My prayer is that your life will not lack God's guidance or direction. It is perplexing to see how many believers, even Christians, can put trust in science, technology and everything other thing, but not God. Trusting God's leading and guidance will never bring you down. It will instead take you to high places of the earth—these are places of divine blessings and honour. Let us get back to God by following His guidance.

Psalm 34:22:

The Lord redeems the soul of His servants,
And none of those who trust in Him shall be condemned.

Divine Guidance Versus Blessings

There is no *want* or lack to them who choose to be led by God for destiny preservation. They will grow strong and excel without sweat! They will fulfill destiny in a grand style with amazing speed in Christ Jesus.

Deuteronomy 32:10-14 (KJV)

He found him in a desert land, and in the waste howling wilderness; he led him about, he instructed him, he kept him as the apple of his eye. As an eagle stirreth up her nest, fluttereth over her young, spreadeth abroad her wings, taketh them, beareth

> them on her wings: So the Lord alone did lead him, and there was no strange god with him. He made him ride on the high places of the earth, that he might eat the increase of the fields; and he made him to suck honey out of the rock, and oil out of the flinty rock; Butter of kine, and milk of sheep, with fat of lambs, and rams of the breed of Bashan, and goats, with the fat of kidneys of wheat; and thou didst drink the pure blood of the grape.

People who get led by God get spared from reproach of any kind. I believe as children of God, the Word of God does not allow us to live in reproach forever? We are called to walk and live in the blessing of Abraham in Christ Jesus. Nothing else! Now, you may ask, "But how do I know I am blessed, Pastor George?" Well, if you have Jesus in your life as your Saviour, then you have the blessing — nothing can change it!

Galatians 3:13-14

Christ has redeemed us from the curse of the law, having become a curse for us (for it is written, "Cursed *is* everyone who hangs on a tree"), that the blessing of Abraham might come upon the Gentiles in Christ Jesus, that we might receive the promise of the Spirit through faith.

The very day Jesus came into your life, you have had access to divine blessings. Even the blessings that God had promised Abraham. Besides, the blessings that came upon Abraham, running down to all generations, are the blessings of greatness. However, divine guidance is the only way to activate God's blessings in your life. In addition, Abraham became successful in life because of his obedience to God's guidance.

> **Isaiah 51:2-3**
>
> Look to Abraham your father, And to Sarah *who* bore you; For I called him alone, And blessed him and increased him." For the Lord will comfort Zion, He will comfort all her waste places; He will make her wilderness like Eden, And her desert like the garden of the Lord; Joy and gladness will be found in it, Thanksgiving and the voice of melody.

I believe the blessing that came upon Abraham was the blessing of greatness and increase. You discover wherever Abraham went, greatness and increase visited him. Look, if you can obey God's divine direction or leading greatness and increase will become your portion. Why? Because inside God's direction is the power to bless you. You can only activate the blessings of God in your life by staying in God's direction.

It is sad to say, there are many Christians today who are afraid of witches, curses of life, wizards, witchcraft and many more to mention. Well, it is an error to live in fear of witchcraft or curses of life as a child of God. What are you afraid of? Of course, people may try to curse you, but it won't work in Jesus' name! Why? This is because you can't curse someone God Has blessed through the power of His love and redemption in Christ Jesus.

Galatians 3:13-14

Christ has redeemed us from the curse of the law, having become a curse for us (for it is written, "Cursed is everyone who hangs on a tree"), that the blessing of Abraham might come upon the Gentiles in Christ Jesus, that we might receive the promise of the Spirit through faith.

Numbers 23:20

Behold, I have received *a command* to bless;
He has blessed, and I cannot reverse it.

No one will stop your God-ordained blessing from reaching you if only you can get guided by God. God's direction is your greatest security of all times in life. What God has said about you is irreversible! They may not like you, but they can't reverse your blessing from reaching you. My prayer is that you will walk in God's divine direction henceforth. Stop listening to yourself and people around you more than you listen to God.

1 Chronicles 4:10

And Jabez called on the God of Israel saying, "Oh, that You would bless me indeed, and enlarge my territory, that Your hand would be with me, and that You would keep *me* from evil, that I may not cause pain!" So God granted him what he requested.

The prayer of Jabez in the above Scripture was powerful! He never prayed for material things, but prayed for the blessing of God to reach him. Why? This is because there is nothing you are looking for in life today that is not answerable to God's blessings. With God's blessings comes favour, divine speed, increase and honour. However, if you cannot get guided or directed by God, it is hard to make it in life. Just be careful!!

Jeremiah 6:16-17

Thus says the Lord: "Stand in the ways and see, And ask for the old paths, where the good way is, And walk in it; Then you will find rest for your souls. But they said, 'We will not walk in it. Also, I set watchmen over you, saying, 'Listen to the sound of the trumpet!' But they said, 'We will not listen.'

Focusing on God's Guidance

Hebrews 10:35

Therefore do not cast away your confidence, which has great reward. For you have need of endurance, so that after you have done the will of God, you may receive the promise: "For yet a little while, *And* He who is coming will come and will not tarry. Now the just shall live by faith; But if *anyone* draws back, My soul has no pleasure in him."

When people deviate their focus from God's guidance, God's hand withdraws from them. Listen, beloved, God can't lead you if you do not maintain your focus on Him or what He is saying to you. He needs your attention and focus! David fought many battles, but lost none. Why? He was a man of divine guidance from God. People who treasure God's divine guidance above everything will never go down, no matter how hard life becomes.

2 Samuel 5: 17-19

Now when the Philistines heard that they had anointed David king over Israel, all the Philistines went up to search for David. And David heard *of it* and went down to the stronghold. The Philistines also went and deployed themselves in the Valley of Rephaim. So David inquired of the Lord, saying, "Shall I go up against the Philistines? Will You deliver them into my hand?" And the Lord said to David, "Go up, for I will doubtless deliver the Philistines into your hand."

How do you ensure you are following God's direction in your life? Of course, there are so many ways such as the Word of God, Inner voice, conviction, dreams, vision and prophecy. However, God's Word is the primary way God leads us. You can't go wrong following God's Word for your life and destiny. The Word of God is the lamp to our feet and the light to our path—that is all about divine guidance. The Word of God isn't it?

Psalm 119:105

Your word is a lamp to my feet And a light to my path.

James 1:21

Therefore lay aside all filthiness and overflow of wickedness, and receive with meekness the implanted word, which is able to save your souls.

The dictionary meaning of the word meekness is also: *humbleness, submissiveness, gentleness, modesty, mildness,* and *compliance*. That is the manner your heart should have when receiving God's Word. It is the entrance of God's Word, and not the existence of it, that makes God's Word effective in your life. Embrace God's Word! It will transform and preserve your life from destruction and the wickedness of this world.

My prayer for you is that you will love nothing but God and His Word. You will not sell yourself to the corrupt and wicked system of this world. Instead, you will walk in God's divine guidance and plan for your life in Christ Jesus.

Destiny Prayer 3.

"Lord Jesus, I surrender my whole life to you. Holy Spirit guide me to hear your voice everyday for direction either from the Word of God or in my spirit."

(Romans 8:14, Isaiah 30:21)

CHAPTER 4

The Word of God

God's Word is Effective

Foremost, God's Word has untold power and fire inside it to preserve your life and destiny from destruction. No devil will ever touch you when God's Word becomes your primary focus. The Word of God has supernatural power to even recreate your own life and destiny in Christ Jesus. Never take

God's Word for granted in your life. It is the only God-ordained tool for preserving your destiny from corruption.

Luke 24:13-15, 32

Now behold, two of them were traveling that same day to a village called Emmaus, which was seven miles from Jerusalem. And they talked together of all these things which had happened. So it was, while they conversed and reasoned, that Jesus Himself drew near and went with them. And they said to one another, "Did not our heart burn within us while He talked with us on the road, and while He opened the Scriptures to us?

The Word of God is effective and has unparalleled power to change things around your life. Look, there was a unique dimension of God's Word Jesus operated from that is recorded in Scripture. I call it "The fire dimension" of God's Word. We can find this dimension when Jesus spoke to Cleopas on his way to Emmaus. In fact, after Jesus left Cleopas and his friend that night, they all confirmed the fire in what He spoke.

Luke 24:32

And they said to one another, "Did not our heart burn within us while He talked with us on the road, and while He opened the Scriptures to us?"

You and I, including this generation, need more of God's Word as never. Apart from that, never question God's Word in your life at all. God's Word remains unquestionable because it is infallible—it has no mistakes—it is perfect. I have made it my mission in life to never question God's Word, even though I do not understand it. Only because I don't want to dispute the truth, which is the Word of God — it is my stronghold.

In fact, the Bible does not lead or instruct us to dispute God's Word, but to know it. Why? Because the knowledge of God's Word will always set us free (John 8:31-32). Without doubt, the two disciples in Luke Luke 24:13-15, 32 got fired up by the fire of God's Word, as Jesus spoke to them. Well, let me submit to you that once you have access to the fire of God's Word, no devil will ever stop your destiny in Christ Jesus.

The *fire dimension* of God's Word is indeed powerful, such that you can earn yourself divine backing from God. Maybe the fire dimension of God's Word here may not sound real to you—well, it is indeed real. In this dimension, supernatural things happen without measure. Now, instead of having doubts in your mind about this dimension, ask the Holy Spirit to help you. He will open up your spiritual eyes to the fire dimension of God's Word in your life.

Jeremiah 20:9

Then I said, "I will not make mention of Him, Nor speak anymore in His name." But *His word* was in my heart like a burning fire Shut up in my bones; I was weary of holding *it* back, And I could not.

Even Jeremiah the Prophet had the same experience where God's Word was like a fire in his bones. Hence, just because you have not experienced this dimension of God's Word, does not mean it does not exist. Each time you question the Word of God, you are reducing the chances of seeing its effectiveness in your life.God's Word does not exist for arguments, but for us to believe it. Only then can it have influence over our lives.

Many years ago, God spoke to me about making His Word in my mouth a fire. Since then, I have seen several miracles and wonders happening in our meetings just by declaring His Word. Why? It is because of the fire of God's Word at work in my life. Hence, don't just celebrate your eloquence of words, but much more the fire in the Words of God you speak. Now, to confirm that word, He gave me the Scripture below:

Jeremiah. 5:14

Therefore thus says the Lord God of hosts: "Because you speak this word, Behold, I will make My words in your mouth fire, And this people wood, And it shall devour them.

Once again, I have several times experienced the fire dimension of God's Word. One day in 2006, I sat down at a church conference with friends during our quick break. Now, as I was sharing God's Word, suddenly the place got charged with the divine presence of God. It felt like an "electric charge" in the atmosphere right where we were sitting. Everyone felt it and was very much astonished, as it was their first time.

Now, to my surprise, I was not even praying, but just sharing the Word of God. I believe that the electric charge was the fire of God's Word. Each time that fire manifests, lives and destinies of people get preserved and transformed. When you share God's Word in faith; the Holy Spirit will rekindle the fire of God's Word. Then, as soon as that happens, the lives of people around you never remain the same at all.

Dominion by the Word

Deuteronomy 28:13

> And the Lord will make you the head and not the tail; you shall be above only, and not be beneath, if you heed the commandments of the Lord your God, which I command you today, and are careful to observe *them.*

The Word of God will always set you above and above only. There is no devil that can stop the fire dimension of God's Word in your life. In fact, it is walking in this dimension of God's Word that establishes your dominion in Christ Jesus. Besides, the fire dimension of God's Word will stop any kind of demonic activities in your life or environment. Hence, it is high time to seek God for this dimension of God's Word.

I believe every child of God today is a candidate for this dimension of God's

Word. I remember one day God spoke to me and said, ***"I will surely cause my words in your mouth to be like fire so that whatever you speak will bring deliverance to this generation."*** That was such a massive and powerful word for my life and destiny in Christ Jesus. That word was powerful indeed, and today I can see the fruits of that same word.

When God spoke those words to me, I took them word for word—I believed them all. Hence, today I can see incredible results or miracles in our meetings. Of course, I see people being healed and delivered from critical sicknesses, diseases, and conditions of all kinds. Why? Well, that is because of the fire dimension of God's Word operable in my life. I pray the same dimension will be operable in your own life, in Jesus' name.

For example, in the year 2004, I prayed for one woman who had a serious chest infection that had afflicted her life for many months. She could not easily get up from her hospital bed and no one knew what to do — even medical doctors. However, the all-powerful and all knowing physician Jesus Christ knew what to do. Then, after praying for her with authority, God healed her in the self-same hour.

I believe the healing itself was because of the fire dimension of God's Word. Nothing else! If you have Jesus in your life, you are a candidate for this dimension of God's Word. I don't know about you, but my heart's desire is to operate in this dimension of God's Word every day. One time, Jesus entered a synagogue and healed someone's withered hand. The miracle was because of the fire dimension of God's Word operable in Him.

Then, in the year 2006, I was holding an anointing and healing service for two people only. Now, as I shared God's Word and sang praises, the glory of God filled the house. In that service, I was teaching about an account in the Bible where the Prophet of God Moses anointed the tabernacle, the altar, the congregation, and the sons of Aaron seven times with the anointing oil to sanctify them and they all got sanctified.

Leviticus 8:10

> Also Moses took the anointing oil, and anointed the tabernacle and all that *was* in it, and consecrated them.

Now, in that meeting, there was a woman who got healed of stomach ulcers. She was, in fact, under a medical verdict that did not allow her to eat solid foods of any kind. She then booked for a medical checkup with her doctor that week—only to discover that the ulcers had disappeared. Jesus healed her! I believe the fire dimension of God's Word is still at work today, only to them that can believe God for everything.

Jeremiah 20:9

But *His word* was in my heart like a burning fire Shut up in my bones; I was weary of holding *it* back, And I could not."

The Holy Ghost and Fire

Acts 2:1-4

When the Day of Pentecost had fully come, they were all with one accord in one place. And suddenly there came a sound from heaven, as of a rushing mighty wind, and it filled the whole house where they were sitting. Then there appeared to them divided tongues, as of fire, and *one* sat upon each of them. And they were all filled with the Holy Spirit and began to speak with other tongues, as the Spirit gave them utterance.

Your life and destiny need the fire of God's Word. Can't you see fire everywhere in the Scriptures? Apostle Peter and all other apostles in the upper room in Jerusalem experienced the fire of the Holy Spirit. I believe the church today needs the fire of the Holy Spirit. Of course, you can contact the fire of the Holy Spirit via the Word of God or baptism of the Holy Spirit. The fire of God's Word makes you an agent of change in your generation.

Now, how do you generate the fire of God's Word in your own life? Well, one way is by meditating upon God's Word with a passion and desperation. I have always tapped into this dimension of God's Word many times by meditating on God's Word. In fact, the fire dimension of God's Word is not something you can generate by yourself. No! Instead, you need the empowerment of the Holy Spirit to walk in this realm.

One night in 2002, I was holding an all-night prayer meeting that started 9pm.

Then, one young girl came up to me and said, “Pastor George, when you were praying in other tongues, I saw fire coming out of your mouth.” Fire in your prayers is a sign of supernatural dominion in Christ Jesus! Now, do you take praying in other tongues that seriously? When you pray in the Spirit, you also invoke the fire dimension of God’s Word in your life.

When the Holy Spirit and God’s Word drench your life, people will see God in you. Now, all that I was doing in that all-night prayer meeting was declaring God’s Word while I spoke in other tongues. Without doubt, you need the fire of God’s Word into your life in order to remain relevant in the school of power. Otherwise, the devil will take you for granted if you don’t have the fire or power of the Holy Ghost in your life.

Exodus 3:2-3

> And the Angel of the Lord appeared to him in a flame of fire from the midst of a bush. So he looked, and behold, the bush was burning with fire, but the bush *was* not consumed. Then Moses said, "I will now turn aside and see this great sight, why the bush does not burn."

The fire dimension in this chapter is the same fire Moses the Prophet encountered at the back of the mountain. Of course, Moses was at the back of the mountain when he saw a flame of fire from the midst of a bush. I believe when you honor God's idea of speaking in other tongues today, you will generate another dimension of God's power in your life. What next? Well, you and I need this dimension of God's Word.

Acts 10:44-46

While Peter was still speaking these words, the Holy Spirit fell upon all those who heard the word. And those of the circumcision who believed were astonished, as many as came with Peter, because the gift of the Holy Spirit had been poured out on the Gentiles also

A story is told of a man of God who one day had an inner urge to pray in other tongues for 8 hours. Well, after obeying that prompting, he then encountered a huge financial blessing in his life. Now, according to him, the miracle was because of obeying God's voice. Well, perhaps with you it might not be money per se, but something else. However, the fire dimension of God's Word is a tool to end all your dilemmas.

In addition, you don't have to pray for 8 hours in order to reap money. No! I am just emphasizing to you the importance of praying in other tongues. Many unworthy issues in your life can find peace and answers through your Spirit-filled prayer life. Friends, life without the Holy Spirit is boring and worthless! However, if you want to live a productive life, then you need the fire of the Holy Spirit—yes, you need it!

Mark 9:23-24

Jesus said to him, "If you can believe, all things *are* possible to him who believes." Immediately the father of the child cried out and said with tears, "Lord, I believe; help my unbelief!"

The man of God, Rev. Kenneth E. Hagin, in his book "The Art of Prayer" narrates of a story of a prayerful young man. Now, this young man, if not with his parents at the farm, he would always go to pray in other tongues on a nearby hill. Then, one day, he heard God say to him that the place where he was praying from was going to be a revival centre. Well, it was such an amazing and extraordinary experience with God.

Now, after many years, that little hill back then turned into a big ministry centre that drew hundreds and thousands of people. The message is that when you believe God and His Word with all of your heart, God won't leave you stranded. Hence, if you don't believe God's Word concerning the power of praying in the Holy Spirit, nothing will change in your life. It is time you experienced the fire dimension of God's Word in your life.

1Corinthians 14:2

For he who speaks in a tongue does not speak to men but to God, for no one understands *him;* however, in the spirit he speaks mysteries.

I pray the fire of God's Word won't just be a theory, but something you will experience in your own life in Jesus' name!!

Destiny Prayer 4.

"Holy Spirit, give me the desire to love and understand the WORD of God. Open my spiritual eyes to revelations."

(Ephesians 1:16-18).

CHAPTER 5

Walking in Simple Obedience

Simple Obedience

What is the *dictionary* meaning of the word obedience?

Obedience, in human behaviour, is a social influence in which a person yields to explicit instructions or orders from an authority figure. Obedience is also compliance with an order, request, or law or submission to another's authority.

What is the *Bible* meaning of the word obedience?

In simple terms, it means hearing the Word of God and acting on it. It also implies aligning your will to God's own will. In addition, it is to surrender to God's authority and His Word with a heart full of love, loyalty, humility and meekness.

Simple obedience will always preserve your life and destiny from reproach. With obedience to God and His Word, your opinion or what you think does not matter at all. If you have an opinion of God's Word, then that is not obedience. Simple obedience is where you don't argue with God's Word in any ways. Instead, all you do is to obey or do exactly what you been told to do in God's Word. Is that simple? I hope so!

In fact, no one should complicate the idea of simple obedience towards God and His Word. Once you do that, then you will complicate your own life without knowing. You have to just follow and do the demands of God's Word without questioning! I see many people having an alternative to God's Word—that is dangerous! Many Christians do their own thing without God's Word. Yet they expect God's blessings. God forbid!

John 2:1-5

On the third day there was a wedding in Cana of Galilee, and the mother of Jesus was there. Now both Jesus and His disciples were invited to the wedding. And when they ran out of wine, the mother of Jesus said to Him, "They have no wine." Jesus said to her, "Woman, what does your concern have to do with Me? My hour has not yet come." His mother said to the servants, "Whatever He says to you, do *it*."

In the above Scripture, the wedding runs out of wine and no one knows what to do. Stagnation, disappointment, and confusion are at their best. The destiny of that wedding must need to be preserved by all means! Every one thought that was the end of it all—they became hopeless amid a hopeless situation. However, simple obedience to what Jesus instructed them to do converted that dilemma into a miracle.

John 2:7-10

Jesus said to them, "Fill the waterpots with water." And they filled them up to the brim. And He said to them, "Draw *some* out now, and take *it* to the master of the feast." And they took *it*. When the master of the feast had tasted the water that was made wine, and did not know where it came from (but the servants who had drawn the water knew), the master of the feast called the

> bridegroom. And he said to him, "Every man at the beginning sets out the good wine, and when the *guests* have well drunk, then the inferior. You have kept the good wine until now!"

It was simple obedience that preserved the destiny of that wedding. There is power in simple obedience! The Word of God is the principal tool for walking in simple obedience. If you can't obey God's Word, then it is hard for you to obey God's Instructions either by His voice or Spirit. The dictionary words for obedience are *compliance, submission, conformity,* and *agreement*. We need to comply with God's Word to see miracles.

God doesn't want you and me to struggle to walk with Him in obedience. No! Hence, He has provided His Word to guide us through life for our own benefit.

Look, simple obedience is not anything more than your adherence to God's Word. Preaching or reading God's Word does not equal obedience. I know many people who read God's Word but obey none of it. It is terrible and sad to see that happen even among preachers.

James 1:22

But be doers of the word, and not hearers only, deceiving yourselves.

If you are just a hearer and not a doer of the Word of God, the Bible says you are deceiving yourself. God cannot reveal the details of His hidden secrets to people who don't want to obey His Word. Many people want the rhema word (revealed or spoken Word) more than they want the logos (the written Word). Sorry, it doesn't work that way! Obedience to the written

Word of God is what introduces you to the rhema Word, which is the revealed Word.

I pray that as you seek to obey God's Word, the Holy Spirit will overshadow you with His power and grace in Jesus' name. There is nothing that will ever beat the power of obeying God's Word and Spirit. Most of the times, when things are not working in your life, revisit your spiritual foundations. Especially the area of obedience to God's Word or instructions. It takes the obedience to God's Word in your life to make things work!

Psalm 81:10-14

I *am* the Lord your God, Who brought you out of the land of Egypt; Open your mouth wide, and I will fill it. "But My people would

> not heed My voice, And Israel would *have* none of Me. So I gave them over to their own stubborn heart, To walk in their own counsels. "Oh, that My people would listen to Me, That Israel would walk in My ways! I would soon subdue their enemies, And turn My hand against their adversaries.

Obedience Attracts God's Presence

Joseph in Egypt was a man of simple obedience. He feared and loved God so much that he obeyed everything God instructed him to do. Hence, God was with him—he attracted God's presence through his obedience and spiritual walk with God. You can't talk about the chronicles of the Patriarchs of Israel and leave out Jospeh. He was a man of integrity and consecration to God. Thus, God promoted His life with amazing honour.

Psalm 81:10-1

The Lord was with Joseph, and he was a successful man; and he was in the house of his master the Egyptian. And his master saw that the Lord *was* with him and that the Lord made all he did to prosper in his hand. So Joseph found favor in his sight, and served him. Then he made him overseer of his house, and all *that* he had he put under his authority. So it was, from the time *that* he had made him overseer of his house and all that he had, that the Lord blessed the Egyptian's house for Joseph's sake; and the blessing of the Lord was on all that he had in the house and in the field. Thus he left all that he had in Joseph's hand, and he did not know what he had except for the bread which he ate.

Nothing attracts God's divine presence like obedience. Failure to live in obedience takes your life down and kills it. Many believers know the Word of God, but very few obey it! One reason God's presence gets attracted to people who obey God's Word is because obedience is one proof you love God. Quoting the Bible does not prove that you love God. Reciting the Bible does not take you anywhere, but obeying God's Word does.

John 14:21

He who has My commandments and keeps them, it is he who loves Me. And he who loves Me will be loved by My Father, and I will love him and manifest Myself to him.

Obeying the Word of God is the only proof that you love God. Jesus can't just manifest Himself to you unless you obey His commandments in love. It is such a glorious and wondrous thing to have Jesus manifest Himself in your life. Mind you, one visitation from God can change your entire life course. I have seen people who were nothing, but after encountering God's presence, everything changed in their favour.

If God doesn't visit your life, then your destiny or future will be at risk. When God visited Abraham and Sarah, Sarah conceived and had Isaac, the child of the promise. Besides, there are so many things that can attract God's visitation into your life, though obeying God's Word ranks top. When Elizabeth and Mary became pregnant, it was because God visited them by His Word. He sent an angel to deliver the Word to both of them.

The second way God visits His people is by the Holy Spirit. Especially if you hate evil and love righteousness in Christ Jesus. Look, God's divine visitations are not free they demand your consecration to God and His Word. Of course, God's visitations culminate in spiritual nourishment and empowerment. Hence, if you want to see a tremendous difference in your own life, then seek God's visitation by His Word.

1 Peter 2:11-12

Beloved, I beg *you* as sojourners and pilgrims, abstain from fleshly lusts which war against the soul, having your conduct honorable among the Gentiles, that when they speak against you as evildoers, they may, by *your* good works which they observe, glorify God in the day of visitation.

God's divine visitations will never leave you the same person at all. I have had many encounters where the Holy Spirit came into my prayer room with His presence. One day, I was in the presence of God praying, then suddenly the Holy Spirit just came upon me. I literally felt a whirlwind around my legs such that my legs vibrated. I could not stand under that power of God—it was a very heavy presence of God!

I believe each time you attract God's divine presence, your life never remains the same. One way to attract God's divine presence is through your obedience to God's Word. If you want to be a man or woman of God's presence, then be a man or woman of obedience. Otherwise, without obedience to God and His Word, you are just wasting time and playing games. Besides, your life won't even change levels in Christ Jesus.

Psalm 81: 10 -14

I *am* the Lord your God, Who brought you out of the land of Egypt; Open your mouth wide, and I will fill it. "But My people would not heed My voice, And Israel would *have* none of Me. So I gave them over to their own stubborn heart, To walk in their own counsels. "Oh, that My people would listen

> **to Me, That Israel would walk in My ways! I would soon subdue their enemies, And turn My hand against their adversaries.**

I pray your desire henceforth will be to walk in simple obedience to God and His Word. Simple obedience will always take you to the top!! God bless you!!

Destiny Prayer 5

"Lord God, help me walk in obedience to your Word as I stay in tune with the Holy Spirit."

(Deuteronomy 28:1-14, Hebrews 3:15 - NKJV)

CHAPTER 6

Divine Wisdom

Wisdom is a Winner

Can wisdom really preserve your destiny?

Ephesians 3:10

To the intent that now the manifold wisdom of God might be made known by the church to the principalities and powers in the heavenly *places.*

Wisdom will always win all kinds of battles, no matter how severe they might be. However, there is always what to do — nothing just happens in this life. You don't just sit down with folded arms doing nothing and expect wisdom to give you victory. No! In Ephesians 3:10, the Scripture urges us to make known the wisdom of God to principalities and powers in heavenly places. Of course, that is your covenant responsibility in Christ Jesus.

In fact, that alone is a lot of work to be done—it is not just an ideology or a theological concept. Nothing just happens in life just because they have to happen. Instead, we have to take our covenant stand against all powers of darkness or demonic entities. Without doubt, wisdom will always stop all demonic activities fighting your life. Don't be that cute and naïve just sitting down without taking your position of faith in Christ Jesus.

What is divine wisdom? It is the practical application of the knowledge of God's Word in every area of your life. For example, when you discover from God's Word that it takes the love of God to make your faith work, then you decide to walk in love. That alone is God's wisdom at work in your life—it is knowledge applied or acted upon! Many Christians mistake wisdom for eloquence of speech. Well, wisdom is none of that!

Another example of wisdom is when you discover that tithe is what you need to walk in financial dominion. Then you decide to tithe into the house of God with a cheerful heart. That alone is divine wisdom at work. What you are actually doing is applying the knowledge of God's Word into your life. Also, divine wisdom is to fear

God, and to fear God is to hate sin with a passion—you stay away from sin.

Ecclesiastes 9:18

Wisdom *is* better than weapons of war; But one sinner destroys much good.

Ecclesiastes 7:19

Wisdom strengthens the wise More than ten rulers of the city.

Ecclesiastes 9:14-17

There was a little city with few men in it; and a great king came against it, besieged it, and built great snares around it. Now there was found in it a poor wise man, and he by his wisdom delivered the city. Yet no one remembered that same poor man.

Ecclesiastes 10:10

If the axe is dull, And one does not sharpen the edge, Then he must use more strength; But wisdom brings success.

Ecclesiastes 10:10 KJV

If the iron be blunt, and he does not whet the edge, then must he put to more strength: but wisdom is profitable to direct.

God's wisdom will always give you divine direction for unusual accomplishments in life. Now, the wisdom talked about here is obtainable from God's Word. There is no other proven source, but the Word of God. That tells me that the level of God's Word in your life predicates the level to which you walk in God's divine wisdom. No Word means no wisdom, and no wisdom means no victory, breakthrough, or success.

I believe the reason people struggle prior to walking in success is a lack of divine wisdom. Why should you go to the city walking, when you have already bought yourself a bus ticket to the city? It makes little sense right there! In the same way, when you have the keys of wisdom to success, why should you first suffer or struggle in life? That is the belief system which has infiltrated both the Church and believers at large.

When you don't have the wisdom of God, everything will be missing from your life. That is because wisdom is profitable and the gateway to success. When you have divine wisdom in your life, it is a sign that you are ready to excel and scale heights of greatness. Each time you turn your back on God's divine wisdom, just know you have just assassinated your destiny. The beauty of your destiny thrives on the wheels of divine wisdom.

Proverbs 23:23-24

Buy the truth and sell it not, also wisdom and instruction and understanding. The father of the righteous shall greatly rejoice and he that begetteth a wise child shall have joy of him."

What does the above Scripture imply? Well, it is all about the need for divine wisdom in your life. Divine wisdom will always cost you something. It is not something that just happens or falls on your laps unknowingly. No! However, when divine wisdom is operable in your life, it will take you to great places your money wouldn't. Divine wisdom is a principal tool for greatness and it has the ability for effortless success.

Proverbs 4:7

Wisdom *is* the principal thing; *therefore* get wisdom. And in all your getting, get understanding.

It is not safe to forsake the wisdom of God, because every supernatural act of God thrives on His wisdom. Where God's wisdom is the power to make a difference will always be present for supernatural acts. Now, how do you gain divine wisdom? Well, divine wisdom has its roots in the fear of God. While fearing God is to hate sin with a passion. Without God's fear in your life, just know that your life and destiny will be void of God's wisdom.

God's Fear Versus Wisdom

Proverbs 9:10

> The fear of the Lord is the beginning of wisdom and the knowledge of the holy is understanding.

To fear the Lord is to hate evil or sin. Thus, the degree to which you hate wickedness in your life determines the rate at which God's wisdom will grow in your own life. However, you don't fear God like you would fear a criminal. No! The fear talked about here is having total adoration of God by hating what He hates. And we know God hates sin.

The story of changing the world starts right here—hatred for sin!

Ezekiel 36: 29-30

I will deliver you from all uncleanesses. I will call for the grain (corn) and multiply it and bring no famine upon you. And I will multiply the fruit of your tree and the increase of your fields, so that you need never again bear the reproach of famine among nations."

I believe you already know that prosperity of any kind is only answerable to divine wisdom. Then, divine wisdom can only answer in your life by your holy walk. Nothing else! Show me a man or woman of divine wisdom. I will show you someone who walks in the fear of God. Look, when God's wisdom is at work in your life, no one can stand your level of operation in life. In fact, no one can even understand you. You become sophisticated!

Ezekiel 36:2

Then will I sprinkle clean water upon you and ye shall be clean from all your filthiness and from all your idols, will I cleanse you.

What I have observed from the Bible is that increase gets associated with holiness or purity. Why? That is because we need holiness or purity in order to walk in divine increase. You may say, "But Pastor George, God is gracious and merciful." Of course, He is! However, that should never be a scapegoat for you and me to walk in wickedness. Hence, we need holiness in order to see God's divine hand of increase in our lives.

Job 22:30

He will *even* deliver one who is not innocent; yes, he will be delivered by the purity of your hands.

If you want God to deliver you from what unjust people have done against you, then prove to Him by the pureness of your life. Friends, purity is the bedrock for our deliverance in Christ Jesus. Nothing else! If purity or holiness becomes your delight, God will make sure He defends your life day and night. He will never love to see your life go down or get devastated. In fact, He will always stand for the upright both in heart and deed.

Psalm 24:3-5

Who may ascend into the hill of the Lord? Or who may stand in His holy place? He who has clean hands and. a pure heart, Who has not lifted up his soul to an idol, Nor sworn deceitfully. He shall receive blessing from the Lord, And righteousness from the God of his salvation.

Walking with God in holiness is the master key to a life of greatness. It will also set you above nations, and you shall be above only.

Deuteronomy 28:12-13

The Lord will open to you His good treasure, the heavens, to give the rain to your land in its season, and to bless all the work of your hand. You shall lend to many nations, but you shall not borrow. And the Lord will make you the head and not the tail; you shall be above only, and not be beneath, if you heed the commandments of the Lord your God, which I command you today, and are careful to observe *them.*

May the fear of the Lord preserve your destiny in Christ Jesus!

Sticking With God

Luke 15:11-13 (KJV)

And He (Jesus) said a certain man had two sons. And the younger of them said unto his father, 'Father, give me the portion of goods that falleth to me", and he divided unto them his living. And not many days after the younger son gathered all together and took his journey into a far country, there wasted his substance with riotous living."

The Scripture above is all about the story of a prodigal son who went away from His father's estate. Now, as soon as he left his father, everything in his life went down. Eventually, he ended up on the streets without direction—impoverished and hopeless. Life became so hard for him such that the only way out was to feed on pig's food in order to survive. I pray that won't be your portion in Jesus' name. Instead, you will live in abundance.

Now, regarding the prodigal son's story, what lesson can we learn from it? Well, you and me we don't have to depart away from God's presence no matter the case. It is wisdom to never stay away from God, your Father in Heaven. One step away from the presence of God will destroy your entire life. One *grave* mistake the prodigal son made was to leave his father, which is symbolic of God, our Heavenly Father.

Luke 15:13 (KJV)

And not many days after the younger son gathered all together and took his journey into a far country, there wasted his substance with riotous living."

The word *riotous* in the above Scripture means *violent, disorderly, unruly, uncontained, lawless, mutinous*, and *rebellious*.

That was the lifestyle the prodigal son later attached himself to—the devil is a liar! Sad to say, even today, there are many Christians who think life outside there in the world is better than life in the Kingdom of God. In fact, some Christians have even given up and ended up joining the world and its systems or operations. God forbid!

Luke 15:13-16

And not many days after, the younger son gathered all together, journeyed to a far country, and there wasted his possessions with prodigal living. But when he had spent all, there arose a severe famine in that land, and he began to be in want. Then he went and joined himself to a citizen of that country, and he sent him into his fields to feed swine. And he would gladly have filled his stomach with the pods that the swine ate, and no one gave him *anything.*

All along, the prodigal son was safe in the presence of his the father, then suddenly, he got tempted to leave his father's habitation. What a mistake! Hence, his life decreased to a level where he got given to eat the pig's food. What an insult! That is exactly what happens when you walk away from God, your Father. You come to a place where you have no option but to accept anything that comes your way, just like the prodigal son did.

Luke 15:17-18

And when he came to himself he said, 'How many hired servants of my father have bread enough to spare?' and I perish with hunger. I will arise and go to my father and will say unto him, 'Father; I have sinned against Heaven and before thee.'"

Look, though what the prodigal son went through was terrible, at least he learnt a lesson. There are certain lessons in life that you can only learn through experience or hardship. Sometimes, I have seen people leave churches and go away in offence. Then, when you try to help them understand the power of staying under a covering, they wouldn't listen. I pray you won't be that person who will turn away from church.

Sad to say, some people don't like the idea of *spiritual covering.* They are a covering themselves and they neglect God's idea of belonging to a church. Hence, some today are confused, disoriented, and broken—they don't even know where they belong. The prodigal son thought he was fine without his father—especially after he had received his inheritance. May you remain humble all the days of your life? Don't get caught up with pride!

No matter what happens in life, it is important to return to God without wasting time. That is because if you stay away from God's presence forever, it is a risk! Otherwise, you might miss eternity or Heaven when Jesus comes back. And we already know that repentance is the only key to forgiveness. Still more, God can't forgive or help unrepentant people. If you are too big to repent, then you can't get saved at all.

Now, is forgiveness for everyone? Yes, it is, but you need to repent and get back to God as quickly as you can. Bishop David Oyedepo, one of my spiritual mentors, says in his book titled *Dynamics of Bible Holiness*, that the only remedy to cure sin is repentance. Genuine repentance will always move God to forgive our sins, no matter how terrible they could be. I pray your ending in life will be better than your beginning, in Jesus' name.

Luke 15:17-24

"But when he came to himself, he said, 'How many of my father's hired servants have bread enough and to spare, and I perish with hunger! I will arise and go to my father, and will say to him, "Father, I have sinned against heaven and before you, and I am no longer worthy to be called your son. Make me like one of your hired servants." ' "And he arose and came to his father. But when he was still a great way off, his father saw him and had compassion, and ran and fell on his neck and kissed him. And the son said to him, 'Father, I have sinned against heaven and in your sight, and am no longer worthy to be called your son.' "But the father said to his servants, 'Bring out the best robe and put *it* on him, and put a ring on his hand and sandals on *his* feet. And bring the fatted calf here and kill *it,* and let us eat and be merry; for this my son was dead and is alive again; he was lost and is found.' And they began to be merry.

The prodigal son came back to his senses and repented. One way to preserve your destiny in Christ Jesus is to make adjustments when you realise you are off-course. Hence, when the young man came back to his senses, foolishness left him and wisdom came in — hence, he repented. There was nothing good at all about the world he envied. I pray it is your time to return to God, your Father—He is waiting for your comeback.

Job 22:23-28

If you return to the Almighty, you will be built up; You will remove iniquity far from your tents. Then you will lay your gold in the dust, And the *gold* of Ophir among the stones of the brooks. Yes, the Almighty will be your gold And your precious silver; For then you will have your delight in the Almighty, And lift up your face to God. You will make your prayer to Him, He will hear you, And you will pay your vows. You will also declare a thing, And it will be established for you; So light will shine on your ways.

May the wisdom of God establish and preserve your destiny in Christ Jesus.

Destiny Prayer 6

"Jesus, since you are the very wisdom of God then help me to gain wisdom and understanding from your presence for my daily walk."

(James 1:5, Proverbs 4:7)

CHAPTER 7

Dynamics of Bible Holiness

The Power of Holiness

There is no life or destiny that holiness can not preserve. Holiness in Christ Jesus has the power to make your life great and secure your eternity.

Proverbs 14:11

The house of the wicked shall be overthrown but the tabernacle of the upright shall flourish.

Then Proverbs 15:6

> In the house of the righteous is much treasure but in the revenues of the wicked is trouble.

Proverbs 3:33

> The curse of the Lord *is* on the house of the wicked, but He blesses the home of the just.

Friends, holiness speaks louder than prayer. When your life gets set apart from the world to follow God, that is holiness. The separation is not something that is done by human hands, but by the help of the Holy Spirit. It does not matter how prayerful you are today, holiness is a must. Hence, you can't replace holiness with prayer—it is ignorance to do that! Prayer is in its own class or category, just like holiness is.

I have seen people who are prayerful but still live in sin. Holiness and prayer are not the same thing—yet they work together. Well, one thing every child of God must know is that holiness is a consistent spiritual walk with God. It has nothing to do with your titles or theological education. No! You may even be a pastor, yet you love wickedness. Insomuch that sin has now become your lifestyle or a way of living. God forbid!

Psalm 66:18-19

If I regard iniquity in my heart, The Lord will not hear. *But* certainly God has heard *me;* He has attended to the voice of my prayer.

Sin is the major blocker of your life and destiny. Hence, most of the unanswered prayers have their roots in sin or wickedness. Unless you deal with sin in your life, God will not pay attention to your prayers. The journey of answered prayer and greatness begins with a holy walk with

God. Yes, if you want God to listen to your prayers, then walk in holiness with Him (Hebrews 12:14). Holiness is not an option, but a must!

John 9:31

> Now we know that God does not hear sinners; but if anyone is a worshiper of God and does His will, He hears him.

Look, if you want God to listen to your prayers, then repentance is the way to go. Without doubt, if we repent of our sins, God is faithful and just to forgive us of our sins. There is no single person here on earth who never makes mistakes, we all do. However, we don't focus on them all the days of our lives. It is a lack of understanding for you to focus on your sin when there is room for repentance and making things right with God.

I believe God loves us despite the mistakes that we have made in life before.

He will never treat us as our sins deserve, because He is a forgiving Father. In fact, out of all the billion thoughts God has about you, you will never find one thought condemning you. Why? Because He loves us and His love is unfailing. However, we are required to walk in holiness as the only guarantee of walking in dominion—nothing else!

Joshua 7:1

> But the children of Israel committed a trespass regarding the accursed things, for Achan the son of Carmi, the son of Zabdi, the son of Zerah, of the tribe of Judah, took of the accursed things; so the anger of the Lord burned against the children of Israel.

Once the fear of the Lord stops in your life, just know that victory will equally stop. That is how serious the subject of holiness is in the sight of God. There was a time in the Bible when victory stopped in the entire assembly of Israel. Why? That was because of the sin the young man, A Chan, committed against God. Hence, the point where your holiness stops is where your defeat with start from in your life. Just be careful!

In Joshua 6:1-27, the servant of God Joshua, had just defeated Jericho, then they lost the battle against a small tribe called "Ai". What went wrong? Well, the defeat was because of sin in the assembly of Israel. I believe where your holiness ends is where your victory walk will end. Holiness is not a fun-fair, but a weapon of war in the day of battle. Above all, holiness is the highway, even the gateway to miracles or victory.

Joshua 7:4-6

So about three thousand men went up there from the people, but they fled before the men of Ai. And the men of Ai struck down

> about thirty-six men, for they chased them *from* before the gate as far as Shebarim, and struck them down on the descent; therefore the hearts of the people melted and became like water. Then Joshua tore his clothes, and fell to the earth on his face before the ark of the Lord until evening, he and the elders of Israel; and they put dust on their heads.

In the above Scripture, Israel fled before the men of Ai and the men of Ai struck down about thirty-six men. Why did that happen to Israel? Well, God was angry with the entire assembly of Israel because of sin in the camp. However, the only answer to God's anger was to repent of the sin which was committed in the camp. Otherwise, defeat was going to continue without end. Repentance is one key to appeasing God's wrath.

People, even Christians, today tolerate sin in their lives and expect God to bless them. Well, it doesn't work that way—you have to remove sin from your life. Holiness must be your lifestyle until Jesus comes back, not just a onetime thing. However, when Israel lost the battle to Ai, Joshua did not even know the wrong that was done in the camp. He was innocent before God, but as a leader, it was his responsibility.

Joshua 7:6-9

Then Joshua tore his clothes, and fell to the earth on his face before the ark of the Lord until evening, he and the elders of Israel; and they put dust on their heads. And Joshua said, "Alas, Lord God, why have You brought this people over the Jordan at all–to deliver us into the hand of the Amorites, to destroy us? Oh, that we had been content, and dwelt on the other side of the Jordan! O Lord, what shall I say when Israel turns its back before its enemies? For the Canaanites and all the inhabitants of the land will hear *it,* and surround us, and cut off our name from the earth. Then what will You do for Your great name?"

Repentance is the gateway to forgiveness and restoration. When Joshua and the elders of Israel repented, God restored back the glory to them in abundance. Without repentance in your life, you will get disappointed with no time. Only because the first step to restoration and victory is humility, which leads to repentance and eternal life. Hence, if you are too big to repent or make things right with God, you can't get saved.

Joshua 8:1-2; 24-26

Now the Lord said to Joshua: "Do not be afraid, nor be dismayed; take all the people of war with you, and arise, go up to Ai. See, I have given into your hand the king of Ai, his people, his city, and his land. And you shall do to Ai and its king as you did to Jericho

> and its king. Only its spoil and its cattle you shall take as booty for yourselves. Lay an ambush for the city behind it." And it came to pass when Israel had made an end of slaying all the inhabitants of Ai in the field, in the wilderness where they pursued them, and when they all had fallen by the edge of the sword until they were consumed, that all the Israelites returned to Ai and struck it with the edge of the sword. So it was *that* all who fell that day, both men and women, *were* twelve thousand–all the people of Ai. For Joshua did not draw back his hand, with which he stretched out the spear, until he had utterly destroyed all the inhabitants of Ai.

There is nothing that will ever change your position in life, like repentance. Eventually, God restored the destiny of Israel after they repented before God. Holiness or the fear of God will always restore back into your life what the devil stole away from you. Thus, don't just keep on sinning or enjoying the pleasures of this world as a child of God. There has to be a point in your life where you have to turn back to God in true repentance.

Secrets to Walking in Victory

Joshua 7:10-13

So the Lord said to Joshua: "Get up! Why do you lie thus on your face? Israel has sinned, and they have also transgressed My covenant which I commanded them. For they have even taken some of the accursed things, and have both stolen and deceived; and they have also put *it* among their own stuff. Therefore the children of Israel could not stand before their enemies, *but* turned *their* backs before their enemies, because they have become doomed to destruction. Neither will I be with you anymore, unless

> you destroy the accursed from among you. Get up, sanctify the people, and say, 'Sanctify yourselves for tomorrow, because thus says the Lord God of Israel: "*There is* an accursed thing in your midst, O Israel; you cannot stand before your enemies until you take away the accursed thing from among you."

(I). Repentance

The first thing that Joshua did after the defeat in the camp was to repent and call upon God in humility. That is the number one secret to walking in constant victory. Anytime you realize something is wrong in your life, don't waste time. Instead, call upon God for forgiveness. Sin of any kind is the entry point for defeat in anybody's life. It is also the entry point for the devil, his government, and demonic operations. Just be careful!

Joshua 7:6-9

Then Joshua tore his clothes, and fell to the earth on his face before the ark of the Lord until evening, he and the elders of Israel; and they put dust on their heads. And Joshua said, "Alas, Lord God, why have You brought this people over the Jordan at all–to deliver us into the hand of the Amorites, to destroy us? Oh, that we had been content, and dwelt on the other side of the Jordan! O Lord, what shall I say when Israel turns its back before its enemies? For the Canaanites and all the inhabitants of the land will hear *it,* and surround us, and cut off our name from the earth. Then what will You do for Your great name?"

I believe Joshua was a man of God's fear. He knew that the only way out of defeat and shame was to repent and ask God for forgiveness.

1 John 1:8-9

If we say that we have no sin, we deceive ourselves, and the truth is not in us. If we confess our sins, He is faithful and just to forgive us *our* sins and to cleanse us from all unrighteousness.

(2). Obedience to God's Instructions

Joshua 8:1-2

Now the Lord said to Joshua: "Do not be afraid, nor be dismayed; take all the people of war with you, and arise, go up to Ai. See, I have given into your hand the king of Ai, his people, his city, and his land. And you shall do to Ai and its king as you did to Jericho and its king. Only its spoil and its cattle you shall take as booty for yourselves. Lay an ambush for the city behind it."

The Scripture above shows some of the divine instructions that God gave Joshua for walking in total victory.

Joshua 8:18-20

Then the Lord said to Joshua, "Stretch out the spear that *is* in your hand toward Ai, for I will give it into your hand." And Joshua stretched out the spear that *was* in his hand toward the city. So *those in* ambush arose quickly out of their place; they ran as soon as he had stretched out his hand, and they entered the city and took it, and hurried to set the city on fire. And when the men of Ai looked behind them, they saw, and behold, the smoke of the city ascended to heaven. So they had no power to flee this way or that way, and the people who had fled to the wilderness turned back on the pursuers.

In the above Scriptures, God kept on instructing Joshua on how to attain and walk in victory. Of course, after you have made things right with God, you have repented and God has forgiven you. The next thing is for you to wait upon Him (God) for instructions or guidance. Each time you ignore the need for spiritual guidance, just know that your life won't go far. I pray you won't be that person who ignores God's divine guidance.

Friends, understand that your victory in life is always a function of God's divine instructions. For instance, if you lost the battle due to sin, then what are you going to do next? Wait for instructions! The same thing happened to Apostle Paul in the book of Acts 9:1-7. After an encounter with Jesus, He got asked to go into a particular city to wait for instructions from God about the next move. Don't just do things anyhow, instead wait upon God.

Acts 9:3-6

As he journeyed he came near Damascus, and suddenly a light shone around him

> from heaven. Then he fell to the ground, and heard a voice saying to him, "Saul, Saul, why are you persecuting Me?" And he said, "Who are You, Lord?" Then the Lord said, "I am Jesus, whom you are persecuting. It *is* hard for you to kick against the goads." So he, trembling and astonished, said, "Lord, what do You want me to do?" Then the Lord *said* to him, "Arise and go into the city, and you will be told what you must do."

Even Apostle Paul had to be told to wait for instructions for the next phase of his life and ministry. Many people, when things are not working, they keep on doing the same thing. Look, Apostle Paul had to wait upon God for further instructions, and God sent someone to show him what was next. Sad to say, today divine guidance is not something that is given attention. Every one wants to do their own thing or go their own way. God forbid!

Acts 26: 15-18

So I said, 'Who are You, Lord?' And He said, 'I am Jesus, whom you are persecuting. But rise and stand on your feet; for I have appeared to you for this purpose, to make you a minister and a witness both of the things which you have seen and of the things which I will yet reveal to you. I will deliver you from the *Jewish* people, as well as *from* the Gentiles, to whom I now send you, to open their eyes, *in order* to turn *them* from darkness to light, and *from* the power of Satan to God, that they may receive forgiveness of sins and an inheritance among those who are sanctified by faith in Me.

Holiness is Non-Negotiable

1 Peter 1:13-16

Therefore gird up the loins of your mind, be sober, and rest *your* hope fully upon the grace that is to be brought to you at the revelation of Jesus Christ; as obedient children, not conforming yourselves to the former lusts, *as* in your ignorance; but as He who called you *is* holy, you also be holy in all *your* conduct, because it is written, "Be holy, for I am holy."

If anyone today wants to preserve their own destiny, holiness is the way to go. Holiness is not just a good idea, but God's own divine idea. There is another account in the Bible where Israel suffered a terrible death experience in the camp. What was the cause? Sexual sin in the congregation! Sin is terrible; do not entertain it please. It can destroy your entire life, destiny, career, or business just in one moment if given room.

1 Corinthains 10: 6-11

Now these things became our examples, to the intent that we should not lust after evil things as they also lusted. And do not become idolaters as *were* some of them. As it is written, "The people sat down to eat and drink, and rose up to play." Nor let us commit sexual immorality, as some of them did, and in one day twenty-three thousand fell; nor let us tempt Christ, as some of them also tempted, and were destroyed by serpents; nor complain, as some of them also complained, and were destroyed by the destroyer. Now all these things happened to them as examples, and they were written for our admonition, upon whom the ends of the ages have come.

Sin will destroy and stop your destiny the quickest if you allow it into your life.

Numbers 25:1-5

Now Israel remained in Acacia Grove, and the people began to commit harlotry with the women of Moab. They invited the peo-

> ple to the sacrifices of their gods, and the people ate and bowed down to their gods. So Israel was joined to Baal of Peor, and the anger of the Lord was aroused against Israel. Then the Lord said to Moses, "Take all the leaders of the people and hang the offenders before the Lord, out in the sun, that the fierce anger of the Lord may turn away from Israel. So Moses said to the judges of Israel, "Every one of you kill his men who were joined to Baal of Peor."

God hates sin, no matter your opinion or theology. Until you stop sin in your life, shame, defeat and misfortune will continue. Now, the grandson of the priest Aaron had a revelation from God that the only way to stop the plague was to stop the sin in the camp. Look, sin will always invite God's judgement or wrath in your life if you don't repent. It is the most dreadful thing to fall in the hands of God's judgement don't even try it!

Numbers 25:7-9

Now when Phinehas the son of Eleazar, the son of Aaron the priest, saw *it,* he rose from among the congregation and took a javelin in his hand; and he went after the man of Israel into the tent and thrust both of them through, the man of Israel, and the woman through her body. So the plague was stopped among the children of Israel.

Amos 4:2

The Lord God has sworn by His holiness:
"Behold, the days shall come upon you
When He will take you away with fishhooks,
And your posterity with fishhooks.

In Scriptures, we see God swearing upon His holiness from time to time. Why? That is to show us how much He values holiness in His Kingdom. I believe holiness is the biggest thing there is in the mindset of God. Hence, anyone born of the Spirit of God today must understand the value of holiness in God's agenda. Where holiness ends is where foolishness comes in. It is holiness that enhances God's wisdom in your life.

2 Corinthians 7:1

> Therefore, having these promises, beloved, let us cleanse ourselves from all filthiness of the flesh and spirit, perfecting holiness in the fear of God.

My prayer for you is that God may pour upon you the desire to walk in His holiness all the days of your life. You can only walk in dominion within God's holiness in Christ Jesus. Of course, you don't need to be perfect for you to walk in holiness. Instead, all you need is a heart for God—pleasing God must be your lifestyle in Christ Jesus. If you decide to make holiness your priority, your life will never remain the same at all.

I pray as you walk in God's fear that your life will change levels of God's glory in Christ Jesus. God bless you!!

Destiny Prayer 7

"Holy Spirit, cleanse my life from secret faults and keep me from falling as I submit my own life and daily walk to you, and show me the steps of holiness."

(1Thessalonians 5:23-24)

CHAPTER 8

Your Spiritual Life

Longing for the Deep

How can your spiritual life preserve your destiny from this wicked world? Well, your spiritual life is a force to reckon with, both in the physical and spiritual world. Hence, if you want to walk in the fullness of your destiny in Christ Jesus, just become spiritual. Your spirituality determines your spiritual command or authority in life. Any time you despise your spiritual life, just know that either your life or destiny will be at risk.

Many people abort or destroy their destinies when they refuse to become spiritual. Each time your spiritual life or relationship with God is sound, you don't struggle to change levels of progress in life. Besides, your spiritual life has everything to do with your relationship with God, His Word, Jesus, and the Holy Spirit—nothing else! Hence, when everyone is rushing for gold and silver, instead rush for God only.

Psalm 55:16-18

As for me, I will call upon God, And the Lord shall save me. Evening and morning and at noon I will pray, and cry aloud, And He shall hear my voice. He has redeemed my soul in peace from the battle that was against me, For there were many against me.

The above Scripture is all about King David's desire to seek God. We all know that King David was a man of spiritual substance and command. He was a man of God's Word, praise, prayer, and divine presence. Hence, wherever he went, God's presence followed him at will. Even today, when you read the book of Psalm, you will sense the presence of God all over you. Why? Because of the Holy Spirit is in what David wrote.

Psalm 119:164-166

Seven times a day I praise You, Because of Your righteous judgments. Great peace have those who love Your law, And nothing causes them to stumble. Lord, I hope for Your salvation, And I do Your commandments.

Preserving your life and destiny has a lot to do with your spiritual life. If your spiritual life is not in good shape, that is already a risk. Your spiritual health ranks top in preserving your destiny in Christ Jesus. Hence, the devil will always fight against your spiritual relationship with God. The closer you get to God, the more spiritual you become and flourish in life. The Bible says something powerful about Joseph in Egypt.

Genesis 39:2-5

The Lord was with Joseph, and he was a successful man; and he was in the house of his master the Egyptian. And his master saw that the Lord was with him and that the Lord made all he did to prosper in his hand. So Joseph found favor in his sight, and served him. Then he made him overseer of his house, and all that he had he put under his authority. So it was, from the time that he had made him overseer of his house and all that he had, that the Lord blessed the

> Egyptian's house for Joseph's sake; and the blessing of the Lord was on all that he had in the house and in the field.

Joseph's spiritual life attracted God's presence and then God made him to prosper in everything that he did in Egypt. One time, he got tempted to sleep with Potiphar's wife, but he ran away because he feared God. Your spirituality is determined by the level at which you fear God. Fearing God is basically hating sin with a passion. Thus, if you want the best of your life, then launch into the deep by seeking God. Life and success are in the deep!

It is sad to see people, even Christians want to reap where they did not sow. How possible is that? Well, if you want a healthy, deep and sound spiritual life, you must need to hate the world and its systems. There is no other way about it! Your value in life is not determined by your material possessions, but by your spiritual commitment to God.

Psalm 63:1-2

O God, You are my God; Early will I seek You; My soul thirsts for You; My flesh longs for You In a dry and thirsty land Where there is no water. So I have looked for You in the sanctuary, To see Your power and Your glory.

In the above Scripture, David offered a deep prayer from the reservoir of his spiritual life. Mind you, David was both a prophet and a worshipper, his spiritual life was so deep in God and the Holy Spirit. He was a prayer warrior and a lover of the Word of God. He had such a deep longing for God and His holy presence. The man walked in the presence and glory of God with such an unparalleled commitment to God.

Friends, the level of fellowship that David had with God attracted God's presence in his life daily. Did David lose any battle in his life? No! Did king Saul's attempt to kill David with a javelin work? No! Why? Because David's spiritual commitment to God was deep. Hence, God sent angels in his way to protect him from the arrows of death. Just remember this! God will always protect your life, no matter the attacks bombarding your environment.

Psalm 121:7-8

The Lord shall preserve you from all evil; He shall preserve your soul. The Lord shall preserve your going out and your coming in from this time forth, and even forevermore.

Psalm 42:1-4

As the deer pants for the water brooks, So pants my soul for You, O God. My soul thirsts

> for God, for the living God. When shall I come and appear before God? My tears have been my food day and night, While they continually say to me, "Where is your God?" When I remember these things, I pour out my soul within me. For I used to go with the multitude; I went with them to the house of God, With the voice of joy and praise, With a multitude that kept a pilgrim feast.

I believe it is that deep desire and love for God that draws God's presence into your life. I have seen in my own life how God has empowered and transformed me. Why? That is because of my relentless spiritual commitment to Him and His Word. Look, the reason for my existence today in this world is God and His Word—nothing else! I don't dream of becoming a politician or anything else, but to pursue God and His purpose for my life in Christ Jesus. That's it!

Your Spiritual Bearing

In this chapter, your spiritual bearing may also mean your spiritual position in Christ Jesus. Now, without a proper spiritual bearing in your life, your life won't see the hand of God. Yes, God doesn't just bless everyone, instead you have to learn to position yourself in Him. How? By God's Word, prayer, meditation, and the Holy Spirit. Each time your spiritual bearing is out of alignment with God's will, just know your life and destiny are not safe.

Isaiah 54:14-15

In righteousness you shall be established; You shall be far from oppression, for you shall not fear; And from terror, for it shall not come near you. Indeed they shall surely assemble, but not because of Me. Whoever assembles against you shall fall for your sake.

Your spiritual bearing has much more to do with establishing yourself in God's fear and righteousness. I believe God can't bless people beyond their spiritual bearing to God. If your life is contrary to God, just know that He won't release the intended blessing upon your life. Instead, make sure you are on the right spiritual bearing with God at all times. Only then will God command blessings upon your life.

Matthew 7:6

> Do not give what is holy to the dogs nor cast your pearls before swine, lest they trample them under their feet and turn and tear you in pieces.

God does not want you to waste His blessings at all. Hence, you must have a proper spiritual bearing to maintain your blessings in Christ Jesus. Look, each time your spiritual life goes down, it shows that you can't handle divine blessings. With divine blessings comes high levels of spiritual responsibility. In fact, you encounter more opposition than ever. However, it will take your spiritual bearing in Christ Jesus to stop any opposition.

It is not like you just get blessed and that's it! No! Without doubt, most of the times, the devil will come and try to counterattack your blessings. Look, if God gave you AUD$100, 000 and you are already struggling spiritually—void of prayer and God's Word. Now, let me ask you a question: what could happen if God gave you AUD$3 million? Some of you having just AUD $3 million in your pocket is as good as killing you before your time.

That is why you have to show or prove to God that even with nothing, you will still get committed to Him. I believe your spiritual commitment and dedication to God will set the pace for divine blessings in Christ Jesus. Sad to say, I have seen people who, as soon as they get a breakthrough they were trusting God for, they stop praying or even going to church. Your spiritual bearing must be constant — regardless of anything.

Habakkuk 3:17-18

Though the fig tree may not blossom nor fruit be on the vines, though the labor of the olive may fail and the fields yield no food, though the flock may be cut off from the fold and there be no herd in the stalls – Yet I will rejoice in the Lord, I will joy in the God of my salvation.

You must prove to God that you are not seeking Him because you want a breakthrough. No! But because you love Him more than a breakthrough or anything in this world. Breakthroughs will come and go, but God remains the same. Sometimes, breakthroughs are for a season, they come and go, but why don't you seek the one who is permanent? God is the same yesterday, today, and forever. He does not change!

Malachi 3:6

For I am the Lord, I do not change. Therefore, you are not consumed, O sons of Jacob.

Maintaining your spiritual bearing is preserving your own life and destiny. I pray nothing will take you away from God's presence. Though challenges of life may come to us, there is already God's divine arrangement for our victory. All you need to do is to maintain a sound spiritual walk with God. Even the flight from Sydney to New York has to maintain its bearing to reach its destination, no matter the storms on the way.

In the same way, if you want to actualize your God-ordained destiny, maintain your spiritual bearing in Christ Jesus. Abraham was a man blessed by God beyond the common. Why? Because he showed or proved to God that he could be trusted. Hence, His spiritual walk and behavior before God were sound and God fearing. You can't stop a man or woman walking with God from prospering in life. God will always go before them!

Romans 4:19-20

And being not weak in faith, he considered not his own body now dead, when he was about a hundred years old, neither yet the deadness of Sarah's womb. He staggered not at the promise of God through unbelief but was strong in faith, giving glory to God.

Abraham gave thanks and praises to God at all times, no matter his circumstances. Running away from God after or before the blessing is a wrong spiritual bearing or behavior. That attitude has destroyed many lives of people. God is not a *Santa Claus* that you only go to when you need things. No! We have to be committed to God at all times. I pray your love for God will not be material based, but God's Word and Holy Spirit based.

The Greatest Answer

Psalm 23:1-4

The Lord is my shepherd; I shall not want. He makes me to lie down in green pastures; He leads me beside the still waters. He restores my soul; He leads me in the paths of righteousness For His name's sake. Yea, though I walk through the valley of the shadow of death, I will fear no evil; For You are with me; Your rod and Your staff, they comfort me.

The answer to lots of problems people encounter today is in their spiritual lives. Your spiritual life carries matchless power to preserve your life and destiny in Christ Jesus. Until now, every child of God goes through challenges, but they overcome by their spiritual lives. I remember one man of God said, "It takes challenges we face in life to experience practical change." Well, no matter the challenges of life, God has a reliable way out for us.

> **1 Corinthians 10:13**
>
> No temptation has overtaken you except such as is common to man; but God is faithful, who will not allow you to be tempted beyond what you are able, but with the temptation will also make the way of escape, that you may be able to bear it.

Without doubt, you need to be spiritual in life, regardless of your opinion. Nothing can rescue your life from reproach, like your spiritual commitment to God. For instance, there is no medicine in the natural world that can heal your financial challenges, but only God's Word! (Malachi 3:10). You can even make appointments with financial planners and advisors, but if you are not a tither, you will still struggle financially.

If you can't use God's Word to overcome financial challenges, then every other method is temporal. There is one divine method I know that will help you get out of challenges. It is actually your spiritual relationship with God based on His Word and Spirit. If you really want to see big things, learn to go deeper into your life with God by hungering and longing for His presence and divine encounters.

The Mystery Behind Carpenters

Zechariah 1:18-21

Then lifted I up mine eyes, and saw, and behold four horns. And I said unto the angel

> that talked with me, What be these? And he answered me, These are the horns which have scattered Judah, Israel, and Jerusalem. And the Lord shewed me four carpenters. Then said I, What come these to do? And he spake, saying, These are the horns which have scattered Judah, so that no man did lift up his head: but these are come to fray them, to cast out the horns of the Gentiles, which lifted up their horn over the land of Judah to scatter it.

Who are carpenters? *Carpenters are skilled traders whose primary work is the cutting, shaping and installation of building materials during the construction of buildings, ships, timber bridges, concrete formwork.* Everyone of us has seen carpenters everywhere in the world working on different projects. Hence, a world without carpenters will be in trouble or suffer. Why? That is because certain entities or works today need carpenters.

Now, just like we have carpenters who deal with the natural, we also have carpenters who deal with spiritual matters. I will talk of the late man of God, Martin Luther, German-born reformer who changed the course of Christian history through one word from God about righteousness (Romans 1:17). He stood on that one word until a revolution was born, and today we are partakers of it. He was a carpenter in His category!

Without doubt, Martin Luther was a spiritual carpenter in his own divine setting or capacity for that generation. The primary assignment of spiritual carpenters is to preserve destinies and generations from corruption. They carry divine insights, wisdom, power, and prophetic words to start revivals of God. Some of these carpenters are prophets, apostles, pastors, evangelists, teachers and many more. What a privilege!

In 2002, I had a vision where I saw a massive crowd of people streaming to an enormous mountain. And these people were carrying white bags, and they looked tired. Then, straight away after that encounter, God spoke to me about the deliverance, healing and miracle anointing that was coming into my life. Did the anointing come? Yes, it did! He also confirmed that word by showing me Obadiah 1: 17-18 through my pastor friend.

Further, in the year 2004, I had yet another dream where I was holding a healing service and the house got filled with a cloud of healing glory, then I saw one woman who was infected with HIV/AIDS come into the meeting and as soon as she entered the building she got instantly healed by the power of God. Now, regarding all these divine encounters, I have seen God use me in signs, miracles, and wonders. And He is still doing it today!

Without doubt, I am a gift to people who need healing, miracles, and deliverance. I am God's carpenter, and wherever people need the help of God, He sends me there by His grace as an agent of liberation. Carpenters are also repairers of the breach! Who are breach repairers? These are carriers of specific answers to the dying world. They are also agents of God's liberation to humanity—they carry the anointing for transformation.

Isaiah 58:12

> Those from among you Shall build the old waste places; You shall raise up the foundations of many generations; And you shall be called the Repairer of the Breach, The Restorer of Streets to Dwell In.

Why do we need the carpenters today? To repair whatever is wrecked or out of order in this world or generation. Carpenters are answer carriers to the dying world by the grace of God. For example, Apostle Paul was a type of carpenter who carried a unique grace of God that saw many lives of people set free from bondages. Another example of a carpenter in the Bible was the prophet Moses, who brought Israel out of Egypt.

Hosea 12:13

> And by a prophet the LORD brought Israel out of Egypt and by a prophet was he preserved.

The man of God, Moses, was a carrier of specific answers to the afflicted people. He was a pacesetter, role model, trailblazer and pathfinder. He carried the grace of God to restore, deliver, and preserve people from calamity and shame. Carpenters or repairers of the breach are also sons or daughters of God, born from the loins of Abraham through faith in Christ Jesus. Are you one of them? Yes, I believe you are!

After reading this book, I pray God will send you to save lives of people. You will be a carpenter sent by God to repair your community, city, country, continent, and nations of the earth. May God preserve your life and destiny from destruction and corruption. Just remember! Your life is not a minus, but a plus. It is not a liability, but an asset and it is not a negative, but a positive. You are blessed to be a blessing and not a liability.

God bless you, go and actualize your glorious destiny. You are more than a conqueror in Christ Jesus today and forever!!

Destiny Prayer 8

"Holy Spirit, help me increase my thirst and hunger for your holy Word and presence so that I can start operating in supernatural miracles and power."

(Isaiah 8:18)

Final Words of Faith

Hebrews 10:38-39

"For yet a little while, And He who is coming will come and will not tarry. Now the just shall live by faith; But if anyone draws back, My soul has no pleasure in him." But we are not of those who draw back to perdition, but of those who believe to the saving of the soul.

1John 5:4

For whatever is born of God overcomes the world. And this is the victory that has overcome the world—our faith.

Mark 11:22-23

So Jesus answered and said to them, "Have faith in God. For assuredly, I say to you, whoever says to this mountain, 'Be removed and be cast into the sea,' and does not doubt in his heart, but believes that those things he says will be done, he will have whatever he says.

Mark 11:24-25

Therefore I say to you, whatever things you ask when you pray, believe that you receive them, and you will have them. "And whenever you stand praying, if you have anything against anyone, forgive him, that your Father in heaven may also forgive you your trespasses.

Galatians 2:20

I have been crucified with Christ; it is no longer I who live, but Christ lives in me; and the life which I now live in the flesh I live by faith in the Son of God, who loved me and gave Himself for me.

I believe you and I can't operate in the supernatural realm of God without faith operable in our lives. For example, when I went into ministry, the first thing God commanded me to do above all things was to operate in faith. Why? That is because faith is non-negotiable in preserving and fulfilling your life and destiny in Christ Jesus. Hence, your race, or nationality, even where you live, is irrelevant—all you need is faith!

OTHER BOOKS BY GEORGE MFULA

- The Covenant Force of Righteousness
- Walking in Financial Dominion
- The Broken & Forgotten Woman
- Understanding the Divine Secrets of God
- The Holy Spirit, His Presence & Works
- Forgiveness
- The Power of Prayer
- The Secret Place
- Nine Pillars of Success
- Winning the Battle Over Fear
- From Prison to Palace
- Plans, Purposes and Pursuits
- The Believer's Authority
- Breaking Satanic Limitations
- Exploits of Faith
- The Incredible Power of God's Word

- Following God's Plan for Your Life
- Dynamics of Bible Holiness
- Unveiling the Hidden Treasures of Redemption

MINISTRY CONTACT DETAILS

Email: riseandwalk@hotmail.com

Phone: +61-425-338-781

For more information

please visit our website:

WWW.RISEANDWALK.ORG.AU

ABOUT THE AUTHOR

GEORGE MFULA is the overseer of Rise & Walk Church, Australia. He is an author, speaker, pastor, leader, teacher and prophet. His mandate is to liberate people from all oppressions of the devil through the preaching and teaching of the Word of faith. His passion is to glorify Jesus and declare him Lord to all nations of the earth through the matchless power of the pure Word of God and the Holy Spirit.

ABOUT THE BOOK

Keys to Preserving Your Destiny is essential to read as it provides exceptional insights to help you grow in God. It will also help you locate and secure your destiny in Christ Jesus for unparalleled results. I believe after you finish reading this book, you will be ready to fulfill your destiny in a grand style. God already set your destiny in motion before you were even born. There is nothing you can do about it, but to discover what it is!

So your destiny and existence here on earth is not strange to God. You may also wonder what destiny is. Well, destiny is the divine assignment which God has put into your life to serve the purposes of His kingdom here on earth. That's why I believe that, despite where you are in life today, God has deposited inside you a unique destiny which is locked up within you, only waiting for you to preserve and fulfill it.

There cannot be greatness without destiny discovery and pursuit! The Word of God is one tool that can help you discover, preserve, and fulfill your destiny. You know, the devil is not happy with your destiny, which is to be fulfilled in Christ Jesus. Hence, you don't have to be ignorant—he is the enemy of your soul and destiny. We are at war! However, it is time for you to arise and pursue your destiny with every strength and passion in Christ Jesus.

Get this book! Your life will never be the same. God is going to lead you into realms of supernatural victory in Christ Jesus. Amen!!

www.ingramcontent.com/pod-product-compliance
Lightning Source LLC
Chambersburg PA
CBHW021143090426
42740CB00008B/921

* 9 7 8 0 6 4 8 3 6 2 5 1 7 *